THE
SACRED
BUTTERFLY

**HOW I UNVEILED
MY AUTHENTIC SELF
THROUGH FAITH AND SEX**

NITAMARIE

Cover Photo by: Jeanette Falu-Bishop
Chapter Photos by: Meghan Lauren Photography
Cover Design by: Kristina Edstrom

PEAK PRESS

An Imprint for GracePoint Publishing (www.GracePointPublishing.com)

GracePoint Matrix, LLC
624 S. Cascade Ave, Suite 201
Colorado Springs, CO 80903
www.GracePointMatrix.com
Email: Admin@GracePointMatrix.com

SAN # 991-6032

A Library of Congress Control Number has been requested and is pending.

ISBN: (Paperback) 978-1-961347-52-6
eISBN: 978-1-961347-53-3
ISBN: (Hardcover) 978-1-951694-38-8

Books may be purchased for educational, business, or sales promotional use.
For bulk order requests and price schedule contact:
Orders@GracePointPublishing.com

Author Notes

Thank you for taking the time to invest in the hard work to unveil your authentic self. I am so excited to start to peel the layers of the veil that may have concealed who you are. This is going to be magical but I think it's also prudent for me to share that this book may include triggers if you have struggled with eating disorders, sexual abuse, assault, molestation, and verbal abuse. Bravery comes in all forms and it will take bravery to face some of these parts of you that want to remain hidden. You will have me to help you and if you want private mentoring to help you become unveiled, please contact me at nitamarie coaching@yahoo.com or you can go to my sexual empowerment website www.nitamariecoach.com.

This book dives deeper into how I transformed myself from a conservative Christian woman who was too shy to speak up for herself in her marriage and business and who hadn't had sex in seven years with her husband into a confident businesswoman who now owns five successful businesses and is a multi-millionaire. I did this by connecting my body to my sexuality through the adult industry.

This book is geared toward all women, to the woman who wants to build more confidence and authenticity, to the everyday woman who wants to reconnect to her sexuality and body, to the aspiring adult model who wants to learn how to become more confident in her sexuality and to the current adult model who wants to learn to become a more holistic person and business owner. Welcome to the journey!

Dedication

I dedicate this book to my twin daughters whom I pray will learn how to be their authentic selves with no apologies when they grow up.

To my mom who has always lifted me in my endeavors, who has stood in the gap for me and continues to be a solid rock in my life.

To my three dads, my biological dad in Heaven, my adopted dad, and my stepdad who have all helped me grow to become a stronger person in their way and have loved me as their daughter, I am forever grateful.

To my friends, mentors, and coworkers who have loved me through the messiness of life and who have made my life so much richer and more enjoyable because of their love and influence in my life.

To my husband who has loved me unconditionally and has shown me what true love, grace, and forgiveness look like.

And to my God who has never left my side even when I have wandered through the darkness and felt alone, you have picked up the pieces every time and have shown me I can finally trust you.

Table of Contents

Love Letter to My Readers

"You Deserve It" may sound like a cliché, but to me, it holds a much deeper meaning. I believe that every woman deserves to experience the big O, the orgasmic pleasure that can be both intimate with someone else and within herself. This type of elation is not limited to the bedroom; it can and should be present in every aspect of our lives. When we tap into our sexuality and embrace our sacred feminine, we unlock a magic within that allows us to create anything we desire.

But how do we tap into this power? My journey of rediscovering my authentic self and my sexuality has led me to discover the answer. In this book, I share my story, practical exercises, and worksheets to help you experience the same awakenings I have experienced.

The first part of each chapter is a reflection on milestones in my psychological development and sexuality. By sharing my personal experiences, I hope to inspire you to explore your journey and discover what brings you pleasure and fulfillment. The additional parts of each chapter include "Keep in Mind" sections and worksheets designed to help you delve deeper into your psyche and uncover your true desires. I invite you to keep your favorite journal and a writing utensil on hand for deeper exploration.

I understand that vulnerability can be scary, but it is essential for true healing. That's why I encourage you to be open and honest in your reflections and not be afraid to write down things you may have never told anyone else. This is a space for you to explore and grow in a safe and judgment-free environment.

Through my journey, I have discovered that embracing my sexuality and experiencing my orgasms has translated into falling in love with my body, my creativity, and my life. It's been a journey filled with ups and downs, but one that has ultimately been transformative. For years, I struggled with self-doubt, insecurity, and a lack of confidence in myself and my abilities. It felt like I was constantly searching for something, but I could never quite put my finger on what that *something* was.

It wasn't until I started to truly appreciate and love my body for all it is that things started to shift. Rather than focusing on my perceived flaws and comparing myself to others, I began to celebrate my unique curves and features. I realized my body is a vessel that allows me to experience the world and that it is worthy of love and care. Through this newfound appreciation for my physical self, I was able to cultivate a deeper sense of self-love and acceptance.

This newfound love for myself extended beyond my physical body and into my creative endeavors as well. For so long, I had stifled my creativity out of fear of failure or judgment from others. However, once I started to embrace my creative side and allow myself to experiment and make mistakes, I found a sense of joy and fulfillment that I had never experienced before. Whether it's writing, modeling, or trying out a new set for my adult modeling business, tapping into my creativity has allowed me to connect with deeper aspects and express myself in new and exciting ways.

Through this journey of self-discovery, I have also come to appreciate the beauty and magic that exists in my everyday life. From the way the sun sets behind the mountains to the sound of birds chirping outside my window, I have learned to find joy and gratitude in the simple moments. I have come to realize that happiness is not something that can be obtained through external means, but rather it is something that can be found within us if we take the time to look for it.

I refer to God oftentimes in She form in this book as Goddess because the Bible was written by men during a time when women weren't taught to read or write. I believe having God referred to in a masculine form has led to the repression of women and the sacred feminine throughout the world. And so it's time to start affirming the She in all things as equal to the He. I believe in the equality of God and Goddess.

I am wholeheartedly a Christian and believe that Jesus was God in human form. He was the perfect Alpha Omega blend of the feminine and masculine sides of God together.

I hope that my story will inspire you to rediscover your magic and redirect your creative energy toward creating the life of your dreams. Whether it's through practicing self-love, exploring your creativity, or finding joy in the every day, know that you are worthy of a life filled with love, fulfillment, and joy.

A Free Spirit Unveiled

A quiet, delicate butterfly landed on the flower next to me. I sat there watching her move her wings softly in a rhythmic pattern. She looked so beautiful perching on the blue flower that I almost wanted to touch her. I reached over to possibly catch her beauty. In as much time as it took me to lean over to the butterfly, she flitted away to the next flower. It's hard to catch something when it's free and knows it's free.

The same can be said about a person who has a free spirit and refuses to be tied down or controlled by anyone. They may have their dreams and aspirations, and they're not willing to compromise those for anyone else.

It could also refer to an idea or concept that's free and open to interpretation. Such ideas may be hard to pin down or define, as they can take on different meanings for different people. For instance, the concept of love is a free and abstract idea that can be defined and experienced differently by different individuals.

Sometimes, we find ourselves in situations where we want to catch something free, such as a person or an idea. We may try to impose our ideas or beliefs onto them, but this can be a futile effort. It's important to recognize that freedom is a valuable and essential aspect of life, and we should allow others to experience it without trying to control or confine them.

Instead of trying to catch something free, we should focus on creating an environment that fosters growth and allows freedom to thrive. This could mean giving others the space and resources they need to pursue their dreams or being open to new ideas and perspectives that challenge our own.

When I talk about being *veiled* in this book, I am referring to the curtain that I chose to put over my authentic self and the sacred feminine within. The curtain was used to protect myself from the rest of the world for fear of being truly noticed, and I wondered if I were truly noticed, would I still be loved and accepted? When I was young, I lived carelessly without my veil, until I was taught that being my natural self was not okay and it wasn't safe, so I started to create more and more layers to my veil until it turned into a hardened mask that took years of healing to peel away.

As I got older, the pressure to conform to society's standards only intensified. I was told that I needed to be successful, get a good job, make a lot of money, and settle down with a nice husband. But deep down, I knew that these things didn't align with my true desires. I longed for adventure, creativity, and freedom.

Yet, I continued to wear the veil and do what was expected of me. I went to college, got a degree, and landed a high-paying corporate job. I worked long hours and pushed myself to excel, all while feeling unfulfilled and empty inside.

It wasn't until I hit rock bottom that I realized something needed to change. I had a breakdown and realized I had been living my life for other people, not for myself. I had been wearing the veil for so long that I didn't even know who I was without it.

So, I started to peel away the layers. I quit my corporate job and started to pursue my passions. I traveled the world, started my own business, and took risks that I never thought I would. It was scary and uncertain, but it was also liberating.

As a child, I was a free spirit. Being raised by a single mother for the first few years of my life, I experienced a lot of freedom—probably more freedom than most parents would be okay with today. But that freedom instilled a kind of magic in my life that I will always remember. I had time to create, time to be, time to pretend.

My childhood memories remain to be some of the most vivid memories of my life. One of my favorite memories is playing in my backyard in our big treehouse and in a secret "cave" underneath our house, which was just the crawl space, but it offered an adventure and escape for me growing up.

The neighborhood we lived in was a run-down part of Denver, the houses were old and unkempt. The backyards were small, but to me, it felt like a fairyland. I could walk in the back with the wild grass growing high and climb into my treehouse where I would play for hours. Creativity abounded; I could pretend to be anything I wanted and somehow I just knew it was real.

The secret cave under the house, in reality, was probably a safety hazard. It was full of dirt and a stray cat who would come around now and then and live under the house. But my brother and I, with our friends, would climb into the secret cave and pretend as if no one would find us. We would bring our "treasures" there to bury them and find later. Ah, the mind of a child.

As a child, I remember feeling free and unencumbered by the burdens of expectations. I had not yet been molded by society's standards, and I had not yet been exposed to the harsh realities of the world. I was innocent, carefree, and full of wonder.

At that time, my soul was not yet veiled. I did not know what that meant back then, but I remember feeling a deep sense of connection to the world around me. I was able to see the beauty in everything, and I felt a strong sense of purpose, even though I did not understand what that purpose was.

I was not afraid to dream big and believe in the impossible when I was young. I was not held back by the limitations of logic or reason, and I did not feel the need to conform to society's expectations. I was able to be fully present in the moment and to appreciate the simple things in life.

Looking back, I realize that my soul was not yet veiled because I had not yet been conditioned to believe I was anything less than perfect. I had not yet been taught to compare myself to others or to feel inferior because of my flaws. I was able to embrace my true self without fear of judgment or rejection.

As I grew older, I began to lose touch with that sense of freedom and wonder. The burdens of expectations and societal pres- sures started to weigh me down, and I began to doubt myself and my abilities. I became more self-conscious and started to hide behind a mask of who I thought I was supposed to be.

But I now know it is possible to reconnect with that sense of childlike wonder and to unveil our souls once again. We can let go of the expectations and pressures that hold us back and embrace our true selves. We can allow ourselves to dream big and to believe in the impossible. And in doing so, we can create a life that is full of magic, wonder, and purpose.

Undoing societal conditioning and reconnecting with one's authentic self is a deeply personal and transformative journey. Listed below are some of the tools and practices you can use to get back in touch with your authentic self.

1. Self-reflection: Engage in introspection and self-examination to explore your beliefs, values, and behaviors. Question the ideas and narratives imposed by society and reflect on what truly resonates with your authentic self.

2. Awareness of conditioning: Become aware of the societal norms, expectations, and cultural influences that have shaped your thoughts, beliefs, and behaviors. Recognize the conditioning that may have led you away from your authentic self.

3. Mindfulness practice: Cultivate mindfulness to develop present-moment awareness. Through mindfulness, you can observe your thoughts, emotions, and reactions without judgment, allowing yourself to detach from societal conditioning and connect with your inner truth.

4. Seek alternative perspectives: Expose yourself to diverse perspectives and ideas that challenge mainstream beliefs. Engage in open-minded discussions, read books, explore different cultures, and listen to marginalized voices. This can broaden your understanding and help you question and transcend societal conditioning.

5. Inner exploration: Engage in practices that foster self-discovery and self-expression, such as journaling, art, dance, or meditation. These practices can help you connect with your inner wisdom and express your authentic self free from societal expectations.

6. Authentic relationships: Surround yourself with people who support and accept you for who you truly are. Seek

authentic connections where you can be your genuine self without fear of judgment or rejection. These relationships can reinforce your authenticity and provide a safe space for growth.

7. Personal boundaries: Set and maintain healthy boundaries that honor your values and needs. Learn to say no to things that don't align with your true self and prioritize activities and relationships that nourish and uplift you.

8. Self-compassion and self-acceptance: Practice self-compassion by embracing your imperfections and treating yourself with kindness and understanding. Accept yourself as you are, embracing your unique qualities and letting go of the need for external validation.

9. Personal growth and learning: Engage in personal development activities such as workshops, courses, therapy, or coaching that can support your journey of self-discovery and help you uncover and embrace your authentic self.

I had to remember this process takes time and patience. I had to be gentle with myself and allow myself to evolve and grow at my own pace. Embracing my authentic self has been a lifelong journey of self-discovery, and each step forward brought me closer to living a more fulfilling and authentic life.

Looking back on my journey, I can see how the veil kept me trapped in a cycle of fear and unfulfillment. It was only by confronting my fears and embracing my true self that I was able to break free and live a life of joy and purpose.

As I shed the layers of the veil, I uncovered my true self. I realized that I had always been a free spirit at heart, but fear and societal pressures held me back. Now, I live my life authentically, with no apologies or regrets. I embrace my wild, free-spirited nature and allow myself to be guided by my intuition and desires.

In the following chapters, I will dive deeper into my journey of shedding the veil and embracing my authentic self. I will share the tools and practices that helped me along the way and offer guidance for anyone ready to do the same.

Keep in Mind

- It is futile to try to control or confine something that is inherently free, which emphasizes the value and importance of freedom in life.

- It's important to notice the pressures to conform to society's standards. When recognizing and acknowledging this, the realization that personal desires were being suppressed may arise.

- The chapter concludes by expressing the possibility of reconnecting with the sense of wonder and unveiling the authentic self, suggesting tools and practices for this journey, such as self-reflection, mindfulness, seeking alternative perspectives, and personal growth.

- There is emphasis on the need for self-compassion, patience, and embracing one's unique qualities while letting go of external validation.

- The transformative process of shedding the veil is a journey, a process, and it may lead to a life guided by intuition, joy, and purpose.

Worksheet

Rediscovering Your Free Spirit

Part 1: Rediscovering Your Childhood Free Spirit

1. Think back to a time in your childhood when you felt unrestricted.

    a. How old were you?

    b. What was your living environment like?

2. What were some of the things you enjoyed doing during this time?

    a. What activities did you choose for yourself?

    b. In what ways did you feel you had the freedom to explore and create?

3. In what ways did you feel supported by your family or parents in exploring your interests and desires?

    a. Did you feel like you could be your true self around them?

    b. If not, what obstacles or limitations did you face?

Part 2: Reconnecting with Your Free Spirit

1. How do you feel about the concept of being a free spirit now?

    a. Do you feel like you still have access to that part of yourself?

    b. If not, what obstacles or limitations do you feel are in your way?

2. What are some things you can do to reconnect with your free spirit?

    a. What activities or hobbies bring you joy and a sense of freedom?

    b. How can you prioritize these activities in your current life?

3. Consider scheduling a "date" with yourself to explore and do something you love, without any distractions or obligations.

    a. When can you schedule this date?

    b. What activity or adventure would you like to do during this time?

Take some time to reflect on these questions and write down your thoughts and insights. Remember that your free spirit is always within you, waiting to be rediscovered and nurtured.

Shame On You

In my young life, I had many life-altering moments that changed the course of my personal growth and development. Some of these moments were significant and caused a shift in my understanding of the world and my place in it.

As a child, all I wanted was attention from the people I loved. I craved their love, affection, and approval. I remember feeling so excited and happy when my parents, teachers, or friends paid attention to me and showed an interest in what I was doing. That attention sometimes led to my detriment.

These moments, among others, contributed to shaping the person I am today. They allowed me to grow and learn from my experiences, and they continue to influence the choices I make in my life. While some of these moments were challenging, they were necessary for my personal growth and development, and I am grateful for them.

In the alley behind our house, we would collect many things as children. My brother, friends, and I often found little treasures like rocks, coins, and shiny baubles around the trash bins and scattered on the ground. We would take those treasures into the cave and add them to the pile of other things that made my childhood magical.

The cave was also a place of firsts for me. It was the place I slayed my first dragon and had a pirate battle. It was where we found the buried treasure (many times) and had Indiana Jones-style adventures. It was also the place where I saw my first pornography magazine.

Somehow my brother and his friends found a bunch of *Hustler* magazines in the alleyway. I remember being fascinated by these magazines. This was perhaps the beginning of my desire to be a porn star, though I don't think I understood that at the time. I think I unconsciously knew I would receive pushback for this desired career path, as well. Something about the taboo act of seeing the nude images in the magazine told me there was something about it that needed to be kept secret.

Girls are introduced to societal expectations from a very young age. They are given dolls, play kitchens, and dress-up clothes, all of which reinforce gender roles and expectations. Even before a child has a chance to discover their likes and dislikes, they are told what activities and toys are appropriate for them based on their gender.

As they grow older, the expectations become more ingrained, and they are pressured to conform. They are told to be polite, quiet, and well-behaved, to wear dresses (but not be sexy, strong, or suggestive), and to always look pretty (because femininity is for viewing pleasure alone). These expectations are reinforced in media and advertising, which often portrays girls as passive and focused on their appearance.

This constant pressure to meet societal expectations can be overwhelming for little girls. They may feel like they have to fit into a certain mold, even if it doesn't feel true to who they are. This pressure can stifle their creativity and prevent them from exploring their interests and passions.

"Shame on you," is a phrase that still triggers me today when I think back to my younger years. As a child, I enjoyed attention and was already starting to feel like a sexual human being. I can vividly recall a moment when I was just seven years old, playing in the bathtub and having my first self-induced orgasm. I never disclosed these "adult" things I learned since anything sexual still had taboo energy; however, as I grew older, I began to experience shame for simply being myself even if I wasn't publicly expressing my sexuality.

What's more, I was never taught what was okay when it came to sexuality. I was merely told what was seemingly *not* okay without explanation, which I embodied as shame. As a child, I didn't know what any of it meant, though it seemed natural and normal to be, dress, and act as I had my whole life. Besides avoiding the things that adults told me were dangerous, I had never before been told to stop being who I was for no apparent reason. Freedom was suddenly confusing.

In third grade, I remember wearing an outfit that I loved—a gray cotton skirt with speckles on it, black leggings, and a cute matching sweater. But when I wore it to school, I received comments from other people about how inappropriate it was and how I shouldn't be wearing something so tight or so short. These comments stuck with me, and I began to feel like it wasn't safe to wear what I wanted to wear or what I felt good and confident wearing.

As a young girl, before I turned ten, I felt the burden of being objectified and sexualized despite my age. I was forced to wear clothing I didn't feel comfortable in, as it was expected to fit a certain image of what a "good" or "attractive" girl should look like. It seemed like no matter what I wore, whether it was a dress, shorts, or jeans, I was still looked at the same way by boys and even male teachers.

This made me feel ashamed and exposed like my body was not my own but something to be consumed and judged by others. It was as if my worth was only determined by my appearance, rather than my intelligence, personality, or accomplishments. As a child, I didn't fully understand what was happening, but I knew it didn't feel right. I felt like I was being forced into a box that I didn't fit into, and I felt powerless and trapped.

The pressure to conform to societal expectations of femininity and attractiveness can be overwhelming for young girls. It can lead to feelings of inadequacy and shame, as well as a distorted self-image. The attention I received from boys and teachers only added to this pressure, making me feel like my body was not my own but something to be used and judged by others.

It's important to remember that every child is unique and should be allowed to express themselves in a way that feels authentic and comfortable to them. We should teach children to value themselves based on their character, talents, and achievements, rather than their appearance. This can help them develop a healthy sense of self-worth and confidence, free from the burden of societal expectations.

At the age of eight, I created an imaginary veil around myself as a way to protect myself from unwanted attention. I thought if I covered up more, maybe the boys would stop trying to kiss me on the playground. This was the beginning of a pattern of self-censorship and self-shame that I would continue to struggle with for years to come.

Despite these experiences, I still loved being myself and expressing myself through fashion and dance. I enjoyed wearing bikinis and short skirts and even did photo shoots with my childhood friends where we pretended to be models.

It was in fourth grade when I created a dance for the talent show. I wore a tiger-printed leotard and leggings and danced with abandon, feeling free and unashamed. It wasn't until after the dance when I saw my teachers' reactions to my "sexy" performance, that I realized my behavior was considered inappropriate. Once again, I felt unsafe to be myself, and I created another layer of protection.

Looking back on my experiences, I realize how damaging and unnecessary the shame and self-censorship were. It's taken me years to learn how to fully embrace myself and my desires without feeling like I'm doing something wrong. I've come to understand that these feelings of shame and self-doubt were the product of societal norms and expectations, which often restrict people from expressing themselves freely.

For a long time, I struggled with accepting myself and my desires, and it was challenging to overcome the fear of being judged or rejected by others. But over time, I've learned the only person I need to please is myself. I now understand I am the only one responsible for my happiness, and I don't need anyone's validation to feel good about myself.

As a child, I didn't fully understand why being sexual and attractive had such an effect on me. But looking back, I realize it was because I needed to feel validated and accepted. And while I now understand I don't need attention to feel good about myself, the desire for validation will always be a part of me.

Today, I'm proud to say that I'm in a much better place. I'm able to express myself fully without fear of judgment or shame.

I no longer feel the need to hide behind a veil or put on a mask to fit in. I know who I am, and I'm proud of it.

I realize that the journey toward self-acceptance is not an easy one. But it's a journey that's worth taking because it leads to a life of freedom, happiness, and fulfillment. And I'm grateful for every step I took along the way because it has made me the person I am today.

By recognizing the importance of self-acceptance, I've come to realize how damaging it can be to hide one's true self. This is especially true for young people and children who are still discovering their sense of identity. The expectations of society and the pressure to conform to certain standards can cause them to suppress their true selves, leading to a life of unhappiness. Hiding one's true self can have numerous detriments, particularly for young people and children who are still developing their sense of self.

First, hiding one's true self can lead to feelings of shame, guilt, and self-doubt. When we are constantly censoring ourselves and our desires, we begin to believe that there is something inherently wrong or flawed about who we are. This can damage our self-esteem and lead to a negative self-image, which can be particularly harmful during the formative years of childhood and adolescence.

In addition, hiding one's true self can lead to a lack of authenticity and emotional intimacy in relationships. When we are not fully honest and open with others about who we are and what we want, we cannot form deep, meaningful connections with them. This can lead to feelings of isolation and loneliness, which can have long-term negative effects on our mental health and well-being.

Furthermore, hiding one's true self can limit our opportunities for personal growth and fulfillment. When we are constantly censoring ourselves, we are not allowing ourselves to explore new experiences or express ourselves in new ways. This can lead to a sense of stagnation and a lack of personal development, which can leave us feeling unfulfilled and dissatisfied with our lives.

It's important to allow little girls to be themselves and encourage them to explore their interests. They should be given the freedom to play with toys and engage in activities that interest them, regardless of whether they are traditionally associated with their gender. By doing so, we can help them develop a sense of self and prevent them from feeling like they need to fit into a certain mold to be accepted by society.

Keep in Mind

- I craved love, affection, and approval as a child, seeking attention from the people I loved. However, sometimes this attention had negative consequences.
- Little girls are introduced to societal expectations from a young age, reinforcing gender roles and expectations through toys, activities, and clothing choices. These expectations become more ingrained as they grow older and can stifle their creativity and self-expression.
- Girls are pressured to conform to societal norms, such as being polite, quiet, well-behaved, and focused on their appearance. This pressure can be overwhelming and hinder them from exploring their interests and passions.
- I experienced shame and self-doubt for expressing my sexuality and being myself. I was never taught what was okay in terms of sexuality, leading to confusion and a sense of shame.

- The pressure to conform to societal expectations can lead to feelings of inadequacy, shame, and a distorted self-image. Attention received from others reinforces these expectations and can further contribute to negative self-perception.

- Children should be allowed to express themselves authentically, free from societal expectations. Valuing character, talents, and achievements over appearance can help them develop a healthy sense of self-worth and confidence.

- Hiding one's true self can lead to shame, guilt, self-doubt, lack of authenticity, emotional intimacy issues, limited personal growth, and a sense of unfulfillment.

- It is crucial to allow children, especially girls, to be themselves and explore their interests freely, disregarding societal gender norms. This empowers them to develop their sense of self and prevents them from feeling the need to conform to societal expectations.

Worksheet

Instructions: Use this worksheet to reflect on your own experiences with shame and self-censorship. Take your time to answer each question thoughtfully and honestly.

1. Do you remember a time that you felt shame for being a certain way? Share the first time you felt shame.

2. The first time you felt shame, how did you "correct" that which you felt shameful for? Were you disciplined in a way that reinforced this shame? If so, how were you disciplined?

3. Did you have more than one thing in your life that you were taught to be ashamed of? If so, what were they?

4. As an adult, do you still feel shame about these things?

5. If sexuality was not listed above, how do you feel about your sexuality? And at what age do you remember starting to feel sexual?

Homework assignment: Revisit the first time you had an orgasm. Was this a pleasurable experience or hurtful?

If you have not had an orgasm this week, give yourself an orgasm with your hand or favorite toy.

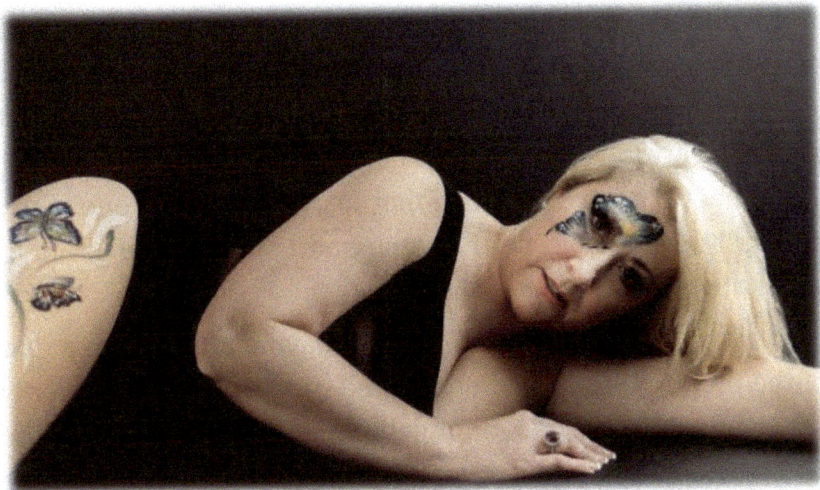

Daddy, I Miss You

When I was twenty-one, I decided to reach out to my biological dad and schedule a time to meet him for the first time. He had never been in my life, and I hadn't heard much about him, but the curiosity to know that half of me had always been there. I had amazing father figures in my life, of course, but nothing compares to knowing your real dad. I needed to bridge the gap.

I will never forget making that fateful phone call to him and how he sounded when he heard me on the other line.

"Nita, wow, how have you been, honey?"

I was irritated that he called me honey after not knowing me for the last twenty-one years, but it was still wonderful to hear his voice. It was deep and raspy and felt like home when I talked to him.

That summer, I planned a road trip across the state to meet my biological dad. When I drove up to his hand-built cabin in the middle of Colorado, I sensed a place of belonging and home that I had not felt in a long time. He walked down the stairs of his log cabin with a twinkle in his eye—exactly like my brother—

and I knew in an instant that I had met a part of me that had been unconsciously locked away. It was with my bio dad that I felt free from judgment and able to let the veil go for the first time in a very long time. It felt safe and having a grounded male figure near me gave me hope that I could find someone in my dating life who could be the same and I wouldn't be afraid to settle down into a relationship.

My visit with him was short, but that day he took me on a tour of the property he owned and talked to me about the butterfly as we overlooked a canyon together. He had a butterfly tattoo on his shoulder and talked about how special he believed the butterfly was because of its ability to transform. He also believed the butterfly was his spirit animal.

I didn't share with him that I also had a connection to butterflies and that my heart longed to have the freedom that the butterfly has to flutter around of its own free will. As I got older, the butterfly continued to be a symbol of my dad's spirit and trans-formation that has been with me always.

During this trip, I saw a sneak peek of what my life would feel like years later, after finally putting the "Daddy" puzzle piece back into my heart and soul. Being only twenty-one at the time, I knew I didn't have the full breadth of knowledge I needed to bridge the gap between my desire to know my bio dad and my feelings of betrayal from him abandoning us when I was little. It would take me until I was pregnant with my girls for me to start to build a bond with my bio dad and for us to mend much of what had been broken early in my life, but reaching out to him was a start.

Even though I didn't know it was a sneak peek at the time, my adult life has mirrored my bio dad's in many positive ways. He lived in the woods and off the land as much as possible. He had a goal for simplicity and being one with his nature. Being where

I am now, I can see how I followed a similar path with having a piece of property to find my peace and how I was building myself up in my exploration of my sexuality.

For me, reconnecting with my biological dad was a pivotal moment in my life. It allowed me to fill a void I didn't even know existed and start to unravel the layers of shame and self-censorship that had been weighing me down for years. Seeing the twinkle in my dad's eye and feeling the sense of belonging in his presence made me realize that I didn't have to *earn* love or hide who I truly am to be accepted.

But even with this newfound understanding, it wasn't always easy to integrate this novel perspective into my daily life. I had spent so many years hiding and trying to be perfect that it was hard to break those patterns overnight. It was a process of unlearning and relearning, and it took time and patience.

I also came to appreciate the importance of the other father figures in my life. My adopted dad, who married my mom when I was three, was the one who raised me, and while he wasn't my biological father, he was a loving and supportive presence throughout my childhood. He taught me valuable lessons about hard work and perseverance, and even though we didn't share the same genes, he was still my dad.

And then there was my stepdad, who came into my life when I was just nine years old. He loved me and my brother as if we were his own, and he played a huge role in shaping who I am today. While my relationship with him wasn't always perfect, I am grateful for the role he played in my life and the love he showed me.

In the end, I came to realize that family is more than just blood. It's about the people who love and support you, no matter what. And while my journey to reconnect with my biological dad was a significant step in my life, it was just one piece of a much larger puzzle.

As I reflect on my experiences with my fathers, I recognize that each one taught me something valuable about life and love. They each played a role in shaping who I am today, and for that, I am grateful.

I can't remember when the exact switch happened to earning love instead of believing I deserved love because I existed, but if I were to guess it was a slow transformation of changing the way I perceived the world. The veil slowly became thicker as I got older. It was as if I was losing a part of myself and I didn't even realize it.

Did you know that if you switch the first two letters of veil, it spells evil? I would agree that being forced to veil your sacred self out of fear of how others will perceive it is being influenced by evil. I might even suspect that the desire to keep women veiled in society is led by the word *evil* plus *D*. Devil.

However, the real significance lies in the idea that women are often pressured to hide or veil their true selves for fear of judgment, discrimination, or even persecution. This pressure to conform to societal norms and expectations can lead to feelings of shame, guilt, and unworthiness, ultimately depriving women of the freedom to express themselves authentically.

Some might argue that the impulse to suppress women's voices and autonomy has a sinister undertone, evoking the concept of evil and the notion of the devil. Historically the patriarchy has used religious, cultural, and societal institutions to restrict women and subjugate them to men's authority. These institutions often rely on the concept of a male deity and the idea that women are inherently sinful or inferior to men, reinforcing the notion that women's bodies and identities must be controlled and veiled.

It's important to recognize that *veiling*, whether literal or metaphorical, has deep-seated roots in the patriarchy, religious institutions, and the systemic oppression of women. By shedding light on these oppressive practices and advocating for women's rights to self-expression and autonomy, we can work toward a more just and equitable society.

Keep in Mind

- Self-censorship and pressure to conform to societal expectations, particularly as a girl transitioning into womanhood, is often the point where many people start veiling their true selves, striving for perfection, and seeking validation from others.

- Understand the metaphor of the veil and the significance of veiling and its connection to the suppression of women's voices and identities. The pressure to veil oneself is influenced by societal norms and can be seen as a product of the patriarchy.

- Reconnecting with my biological dad allowed me to fill a void I didn't know existed and to begin unraveling the layers of shame and self-censorship. I learned that I didn't have to earn love or hide my true self to be accepted.

- Family is more than blood and family extends beyond biological connections. It encompasses those who provide love and support unconditionally. Reconnecting with my biological dad was just one piece of a larger puzzle in my journey.

Worksheet

1. What is your relationship with your parents like? Describe them in four words.

2. Would you consider yourself close to your parents?

3. Do you have multiple parental figures in your life?

    a. Which one are you closest to?

4. Do your biological parents know everything about you?

    a. If not, what areas of your life are you not comfortable sharing with them? If you do not have a relationship with your biological parents, answer this question in terms of the parental figure you are closest to.

5. Have you ever felt like a part of you was missing?

    a. If so, how did it affect your life?

    b. Have you ever felt like you needed to be perfect to earn love or acceptance from others?

    c. How did this affect your self-worth?

6. Do you have any relationship with your parents?

    a. If not, have you ever thought about reaching out to them?

7. If you do have a relationship with your parents, how has it impacted your life?

8. Have you ever felt a sense of belonging or home with someone who is not related to you by blood?

    a. If so, who was this person and how did they make you feel?

9. Think about someone in your life who has played a parental role for you, whether it's your biological family, adopted family, stepparents, or another significant person.

Write down three things you appreciate about this person and how they have impacted your life.

Homework assignment: If your parents are living and you have a good relationship with them, plan a parent/child date, either virtual or in person.

Star Light, Star Bright May I Have This Love I Wish for Tonight

The yearning for love and acceptance is a basic human need. As a child, I longed for the loving embrace of all of my father figures, but especially my biological father. I wanted to tell him about my day, to feel the warmth of his love, and to hear him say, "I love you" and "I'm proud of you." However, my father was distant and I didn't have an emotional connection with him like I did with my mother. This void stayed with me for a long time, and as I grew up, I found myself looking for love and validation in men who were not the best match for me.

I was willing to sacrifice myself for what *appeared* to be love. Because of my upbringing, I had been taught that love from men was supposed to be distant with little affection. I learned to look for partners who showed me "love" in the same way my father had.

Despite the experiences I had growing up, every night, I wished for a long and loving relationship with a man who would show me the affection that I craved. However, I eventually came to realize that I could never be in a loving relationship with someone else until I fell in love with myself. But how could I do that when I was scared to be alone? How could I fall in love with myself when I didn't want to be with myself?

The veil that I had worn for so long became a security blanket that I clung to, even though it had become suffocating. It was like a mask that I was afraid to remove because I was uncertain of what I would find underneath. As time passed, the weight of the veil became heavier and heavier until it was almost unbearable. It was like carrying around a heavy burden that I couldn't put down. But the thought of taking off the veil was terrifying because it would expose me to the world without any cover, without any protection. I was afraid of being vulnerable and open, of being judged and rejected.

But deep down, I knew that I needed to remove the veil to truly discover who I was and what I was capable of. It was only by shedding the layers that I had built up over the years that I could begin to see the real me underneath. It was a difficult journey, but one that was necessary for my growth and self-discovery.

As a teenager, my hormones were raging, and I experienced the same boy-craziness that every teenager goes through. As I reflect on that period of my life, I realize I was experiencing a very twisted and distorted perception of love, which was more like desperation and infatuation masking as love in my mind. At the time, I was in a relationship with someone much older than me, and the dynamic between us was far from healthy. We had a toxic and codependent relationship that was fueled by manipulation and control, which I wrongly interpreted as love.

To make matters worse, this person was intertwined with my social and familial circles, and it felt like there was no escape from the relationship. I couldn't just walk away and cut off all ties because it would have caused a rift in my life that I didn't want to be responsible for—or rather, I was *scared* to be responsible for it. So, I felt trapped and powerless to leave. No one told me it was okay for me to put myself and my safety first. I had only been taught to look out for others and being with this man while I was a teenager was just another example of trying to fill in the relationship voids left by my differing relationships with my fathers.

Despite the warning signs and red flags, I convinced myself that this was what love was supposed to feel like—the constant push and pull, the highs and lows, the drama and chaos. I believed that if I just stuck it out and loved this person hard enough, everything would work out in the end. But the truth was that I was stuck in a destructive cycle that was doing more harm than good.

The other person would ask me for sexual favors and be nice to me in the process of asking for them. However, when we were spending time together, he would emotionally abuse me— calling me names, bullying me, and making me feel insignificant and inferior.

I wanted his bullying and anger toward me to stop, and I would always agree to whatever sexual favors he asked for because, at least for that short period, he was nice to me. This was the beginning of the perverted way that I experienced love. I started to believe that if a man showed sexual interest in me, he loved me.

I wasn't taught that having a physical interest in someone does not necessarily equate to love. This is for several reasons. First, love is a complex emotion that encompasses more than just physical attraction. Love involves a deep emotional connection, respect, trust, and a desire to prioritize the other person's well-being and happiness. Physical interest, on the other hand, is often driven by attraction to someone's physical appearance or attributes, without necessarily involving any of the deeper emotional aspects of love.

Additionally, physical interest can be fleeting and often lacks the commitment and dedication that are required to sustain a long-term, loving relationship. A man can have a physical interest in a woman without any intention of pursuing a long-term relationship or considering her emotional needs and desires.

Moreover, it is important to recognize that sexual desire or attraction can also stem from objectification or the desire to use someone solely for one's pleasure or benefit, without regard for their feelings or well-being. In such cases, the man may not truly love the woman but rather view her as a means to fulfill his desires. In this instance, my partner was using me as a sex toy, and I couldn't see it.

It wasn't until years later that I realized how distorted my view of love was. I had been seeking validation from others, hoping that they would love me and make me feel whole. I was searching for love outside of myself, but what I needed was self-love. I needed to learn to love and accept myself for who I was, flaws and all.

It took a lot of work, but I eventually learned to remove the veil that I had been hiding behind for so many years. The veil looked like tension and stress on my body and held me in a constant state of feeling like a fraud in my own body. I faced my fears and spent time alone with myself, learning who I was and what I wanted out of life. I discovered my strengths and weaknesses, and I learned to love and accept myself for who I was.

Now, when I wish upon a star, I wish for the strength to continue loving myself, and for the courage to continue seeking out healthy relationships that add to my happiness and well-being. I have learned that self-love is the foundation for all healthy relationships, and I am grateful for the lessons that have brought me to where I am today.

Keep in Mind

- Our emotional patterns and modes of connecting often stem from our earliest and most fundamental relationships, like our parents.

- You can only have a healthy loving relationship with someone else after falling in love with yourself.

- It's easy for our masks to become our security blankets even though they may also be suffocating and stifling.

- If we experience toxic behaviors early in life, it can be difficult to separate positive emotions from that behavior. I believed love was manipulative for a long time before I did the work to uncover that my early experiences were not love but abuse.

- I mistakenly associated sexual interest with love, not recognizing the complexity of love beyond physical attraction.

- Self-love became the foundation for seeking healthy relationships that contribute to my happiness.

- It's important to be grateful for the lessons learned and emphasize the significance of self-love in your life.

Worksheet

1. Have you ever been assaulted or abused? Circle one: YES or NO

2. If you circled YES, share the instances that you remember. Remember you are safe here, no one else is reading this but you.

3. Have there been times in your life when you have minimized abuse because you didn't want to cause problems in social circles or within your family? If so, share those times that you have minimized your abuse.

4. Do you enjoy looking and feeling sexual? Circle one: YES or NO

5. Do you enjoy looking and feeling sexual even if no one else sees you? Circle one: YES or NO

6. If the answer is NO to any of the above questions, why do you suppose that is?

7. If the answer is NO to any of the above questions and you answered YES you have been abused or assaulted, did you notice a correlation between when you stopped enjoying looking and feeling sexual to the same time frame of when you were abused? Circle one: YES or NO

8. Do you believe you deserve to look and feel pretty? Circle one: YES or NO

9. Share times when you have gotten pretty and dressed up just for you to see and no one else.

10. Write a love letter to yourself as if you are a secret admirer and adore yourself from a distance.

The Break

The night of my first date with a new boy from the same town as my adopted dad was meant to be exciting and fun, but it ended up being the start of a traumatic experience that changed my life forever. As he touched me, I felt myself leaving my body, and I started screaming uncontrollably. I freaked him out to the point that he immediately drove me home to my adopted dad's house. It was there that I started having visions of people in my room with me saying things that no one could understand.

This was the beginning of a spiritual awakening that was brought on by trauma and can happen because intense experiences such as trauma can cause a person to question their beliefs and view of the world. Trauma has the power to shatter a person's sense of identity, safety, and purpose, which can lead to a deep search for meaning and understanding. And this search can ultimately lead to a spiritual awakening where the person finds a new sense of purpose, connection to something greater than themselves, and a new understanding of their place in the world. Trauma can also bring about a sense of vulnerability and openness that allows a person to be more receptive to spiritual experiences and growth. (It is important to note, however, that while trauma can be a catalyst for spiritual awakening, it is not necessary or desirable for every-one, and seeking professional help to process and heal from trauma is important.)

It was also the beginning of a very isolating time in my sixteen-year-old life. Instead of being surrounded by my family during a time when I needed them the most, I was admitted to the teen mental ward at the local hospital. Group therapy and individual therapy seemed pointless, and I couldn't understand why I was under the microscope of doctors and psychiatrists. I was in a daze, trying to make sense of why I was there. I realized I had not used my voice and advocated for myself for so long that I couldn't hold back any longer. I needed help and I needed to get away from the situations that were hurting me.

After a week of being hospitalized, I was released, but instead of going back to live with my mom, I was told I would be living with my adopted dad and stepmom for a year. While this was meant to be a move to protect me, it made me feel insecure and unsafe. I was put into a school system that was completely different from what I had known and with completely new peers in class. My adopted dad had a different parenting style than my mom, and I often found myself unsure of how to act. I was also attending weekly therapy sessions, which made me feel as if I was broken and definitely not okay.

Of course, this was a time before therapy had mainstreamed and it was mostly used for diagnoses instead of a safe space to talk to people. Because I was also amid a spiritual awakening, I was left with so many questions and no one to answer them, especially not with people in the medical field who steer as far away from holistic and spiritual practices as possible.

I struggled to find my place in this new environment. If I placed the veil more thickly over my face then perhaps I would not be noticed. Perhaps I would just fade away and I wouldn't feel this pain of being alone and feeling helpless.

The inability to control my surroundings made me turn inward, trying to control the way I looked and the amount of food I ate. I didn't want to feel my curves or my body, so I ate less and worked out more. If I exercised more, I wouldn't feel the emotions of loneliness and insecurity. I didn't want to feel my stomach, and if I got thinner, I wouldn't feel my presence, either. This was the beginning of my eating disorder.

Living with my adopted dad and stepmom was challenging, and I often felt like an outsider in my own life. But looking back, I realize that this was a necessary break from my old life. It gave me the space to process my trauma and begin to heal. While it was a difficult time, it was also a time of growth and transformation.

In the end, my mental health crisis allowed me to reinvent myself and start over. It was a chance to shed the old me and become someone new, someone stronger and more resilient. I started to see the connection between the physical world and the spiritual world and how things are connected and nurtured during this time in my life, even if it was hard. And for that, I will always be grateful.

Keep in Mind

- A traumatic experience can cause you to feel disconnected from your body and have disturbing visions.

- Trauma can lead to a spiritual awakening by challenging beliefs and prompting a search for meaning and understanding.

- Developing an eating disorder is an unhealthy way to control your surroundings and numb your emotions.

- Sometimes a breakdown can allow you to reinvent yourself and become stronger and more resilient.

Worksheet

1. Have you ever had an intense emotional experience that caused you to withdraw from society and your regular routines for some time?

2. If the answer is yes, what events led up to your "break"?

3. Do you find that certain events, people, or circumstances in your life trigger you today? Share some of these triggers.

4. Did you have support during this difficult time of your life? And have you forgiven yourself?

Homework Assignment

Visualization Exercise: Revisit the time in your life when you hit rock bottom and had a mental health crisis. Visualize yourself in that state of weakness and start talking to her.

1. What is she most afraid of?

2. Let her know that it will be okay. What words of comfort and encouragement do you offer her?

3. Let her know that she will be stronger in life because of the transformation she is going through now. What advice do you give her to help her navigate this difficult time?

4. Assure her that her future self will be a badass capable of handling anything that comes her way. What positive things can you tell her about her future self?

5. Let her know that if she gets scared again, it is okay to ask for help. What steps can she take to seek help when she needs it?

6. Give this part of you a hug and wipe away her tears. What words of love and compassion do you offer her?

To Eat or Not to Eat

The relationship we have with our bodies can be complicated, and for many, it can be a source of pain and struggle. This was certainly the case for me when I developed an eating disorder at the age of seventeen. It all started with a simple question, "Have I gained weight recently?" The affirmative from my friend was all I needed to hear before I was on a mission to control every aspect of my eating and exercise routine.

At the time, it felt like a way to gain control over my life, to prove that I was strong and capable of achieving perfection. When I strived for perfection, I set impossibly high standards for myself. No matter how much I achieved or how well I performed, it was never enough. I constantly criticized myself and felt like a failure if I fell short of my expectations. But in reality, my disordered thoughts were a slippery slope that led me down a path of self-destruction. I lost a significant amount of weight, my body began to shut down, and my emotional well-being suffered greatly.

It's hard to describe the level of control that an eating disorder can exert over your life. It consumes your thoughts, energy, and time, leaving little room for anything else. I remember waking up early in the morning to work out before school, skipping breakfast, and surviving on a few rice cakes for lunch. My goal was to eat as little as possible and burn as many calories as I could.

It wasn't until I hit rock bottom in college that I realized how much my eating disorder had taken from me. On Christmas Eve, I found myself shaking uncontrollably, unable to calm down or focus on anything other than my fear of gaining weight. It was a moment of clarity that made me realize I couldn't go on like that any longer. I needed help.

I prayed to Goddess to take away my eating disorder, to release me from the stronghold that had taken over my life. And on that day, I felt something shift inside me. It wasn't an instant cure, but it was the beginning of a journey toward healing and recovery.

However, just because I had released the grip of my eating disorder, it didn't mean that my relationship with food and my body was suddenly healthy. It took years of work and intro-spection to learn to love and accept myself fully. Even after I stopped controlling what I ate and stopped counting calories and exercising excessively, I often felt disconnected from my body and would make efforts to not connect with how I felt.

It wasn't until later in life, after my divorce from my first husband, that I found true empowerment with my body and my sexuality. It was a process of learning to love and accept myself for who I was, without judgment or shame. I realized that my worth wasn't tied to my weight or my appearance, but rather to my inner strength and resilience.

Having an eating disorder is a silent disease, one that often goes unnoticed and unacknowledged. But it's important to recognize that it's a real struggle and one that can have serious consequences if left untreated. If you or someone you know is struggling with an eating disorder, please seek help. You don't have to go through it alone. There is hope, and there is healing available.

Keep in Mind

- Notice when your relationship with food and your body is verging on unhealthy, especially marked by restrictive eating and excessive exercise.
- The journey toward healing and recovery is a gradual process that often requires years of work and introspection.
- Eating disorders are often silent and unrecognized, but they are real struggles with serious consequences.
- It is important to seek help if you or someone you know is struggling with an eating disorder as there is hope and healing available.

Worksheet

1. On a scale of 1-10, what is your comfort level with your body? (1 is not comfortable at all, while 10 is the most comfortable you could be!)

2. What do you love most about your body?

3. What do you dislike about your body?

4. Are there ways in which you obsess about how much you eat?

5. In what ways do you count calories or calculate how much fat intake you are getting?

6. How do you eat to feel healthy and good, or how do you eat to lose weight?

7. How often do you work out? Is this balanced with rest days, stretching, and strength training, along with cardio?

8. In what ways do you participate in disordered eating?

9. When you look in the mirror, do you feel like you look fatter than you are?

These are all reflective questions to ask yourself in relationship with your body. If you have become obsessive about calories, food control, working out, or use throwing up or laxatives as a way to feel thinner, it may be time to seek help with an eating disorder. It is healthy to get exercise and to be aware of what you put in your body, but when calorie counting and working out become a part-time job, it has become a distraction from what your true self needs, which is love and connection. It is okay to admit that you want to break free from this stronghold in your life just like anyone else addicted to a drug might need help. It doesn't make you weak or less than to admit you need help. Seek a health practitioner or a holistic health and wellness professional for ways to break free from the eating disorder addiction.

Homework Assignment: Find a place where you can be alone and uninterrupted and turn on some of your favorite music while doing a strip tease for yourself in front of a mirror. Look at yourself in lust as if you were a man paying for a strip show. Do all the moves, slowly undressing, waving your boobs, and shaking your butt.

Journal after your dance: How did it make you feel? Could you get through it without laughing? Did you look at yourself in lust or disgust?

This Hurts…

As a young woman in my teens, I bounced around between boyfriends, I often found myself in many relationships at once depending on what I was feeling and who the flavor of the month was. It was easy to have flings, but I was also in a space where I wouldn't allow myself to go deep enough emotionally to care about our partnership either.

The abandonment I felt from the revolving door of father figures in my youth gave me the perspective that men were not worth getting attached to because they wouldn't care about me enough to work things out and stay, so it was safer for me to just *not* form an attachment in the first place.

I slept with men because I could, and by the time I was eighteen and in college, I had developed enough sexual prowess that I could land any man I wanted. After a while of little to no connection, the boredom eventually caught up to me and my days of sleeping around changed when I started dating some-one at age twenty-two while working at Walt Disney World®.

Working at Disney was what I consider to be my first big adventure as a brand-new adult. I no longer lived with my parents, and I was finished with college. Life was happening for me at The Happiest Place on Earth. I was so excited to spread my wings and experience the opportunities that awaited me. Little did I know that my own Achilles heels titled *men* and *codependence* would prevent me from truly finding myself or experiencing all that I truly could have if I had just remained single.

My first serious relationship happened at a time when I craved human connection and the stability of a collaborative partner. When I moved to Orlando, I didn't have anyone around and my family were all far enough away that I couldn't just drive to them if I wanted to. I stepped into my newfound freedom determined to make a relationship work since I had a fresh start and a clean slate. No one knew who I was in Florida. It was my chance to drop some of my veil and make a name for myself that was more in line with who I truly wanted to be.

Unfortunately, this relationship turned out to be toxic, and I found myself trapped in a cycle of emotional and verbal abuse that I was unable to break free from for a long time. I started dating someone who within weeks had moved into my apartment with me. I paid the bills when he didn't have the money, which was often since he couldn't hold down a job. I went into debt paying for his music gear when he couldn't afford it. I overlooked his abuse and even the idea that he could be cheating on me.

At first, I overlooked the small red flags that appeared at the beginning of the relationship, such as his lack of employment and his disrespectful behavior toward me. However, as time went on, these red flags turned into hurtful attacks that I could no longer ignore. Despite the abuse, I was determined to make the relationship work because I had never been attached to any man before, and I thought this was what love was supposed to be.

It was not until one day, after Goddess woke me up to the abuse, that I realized I needed to leave and that I deserved more. I was walking home one day from work and opened up a bill I had racked up in the relationship and realized I was not only being taken advantage of but I was also being stepped on along the way. It was almost as if God yelled at me from Heaven saying "Nita!!! What in the world are you doing?? Get out of this situation now!!"

After securing the new job and apartment, I brought the release form to my ex to sign me off our lease and let me go live my life without him. I knew God was on my side as my ex didn't put up a fuss and signed the papers. However, at the grocery store later that evening, we got into a huge fight and I knew that was my chance to escape. I left my ex at the store and rushed home to pack my things, but he arrived sooner than I could get everything and leave.

My ex came barreling through the door and immediately started shouting and throwing things at me. I dodged a huge mirror that crashed down beside me as I swept up what I could carry and bolted. Outside, he chased me and jumped onto my car as I was making my getaway. I was able to swerve enough that he slid off my car and I sped down the road and away.

Since this was 1999, I had to pull off to find a phone, paranoid the whole time that he was chasing me and coming to hurt me. I found a gas station and called my parents in hysterics, begging them to help me.

Luckily, they bought me a night at a hotel and were able to calm me down, but I realized I wouldn't be able to stay in Florida with the constant fear hanging over me. So, I called the police to escort me back to my apartment to get the rest of my things and hit the road to my parents' house in Virginia.

Even though the police were there, I was rushing so much that I unfortunately left my two cats behind, but I had reclaimed my own "pussycat" in the form of my freedom and safety.

Looking back, I realize that I wasted so much time, money, and heartache trying to make a toxic relationship work. I stopped pursuing my dreams and cut off other opportunities to try and save the relationship. If only I had been able to remain single, I could have focused on building myself as a model and entertainer at a young age. However, I didn't have the confidence to be alone and pursue my dreams. I stopped pursuing my dreams of being a "good girlfriend," and I cut off other opportunities to try and save the relationship.

In the end, I learned valuable lessons from this experience, and I am grateful for them. But I will never get that time of my life back. I now know that everything happens in divine time, and Goddess knew that I had other things to learn. Her timing was still perfect for me, at any age.

Keep in Mind

- Notice where you are unattached to any particular connection or relationship.
- Just because you desire human connection and stability, doesn't mean you should enter into a toxic relationship.
- Recognize the wasted time, money, and heartache in trying to save a toxic relationship and sacrificing your dreams for this person who isn't aligned with your highest good.
- The experience taught valuable lessons, emphasizing the importance of divine timing and personal growth.

Worksheet

1. Have you ever been with someone who has verbally, emotionally, or physically abused you?

2. Did you recognize this as abuse right away?

3. What is your threshold for what you accept verbally, emotionally, or physically in a relationship? Do you have high standards and address things immediately when someone hurts you? Or do you brush them off as acceptable, hoping to keep the peace?

Abuse can happen in any relationship. It does not need to be an intimate relationship. It can happen between siblings, parent/child, child/parent, between friends, and coworkers. Having high standards means having high standards in all relationships.

Homework Assignment:

1. Write down a time in your journal when you were abused. (Every woman has been abused at some point in her life either within a relationship or by a stranger. We brush it off as okay, but the scar is still there.)

2. How did this abuse make you feel?

3. Did you address it with the other person?

4. Are you still in some sort of relationship with this person?

Oftentimes times abusive behavior can be transformed. However, both parties need to be committed to personal growth and awareness. It can be very healing to transform abusive behavior between two willing parties. However, seek guidance so you are not blinded by the honeymoon stage of the abuse cycle, and both parties are committed to true change.

Instructions: Answer the questions above and reflect on your answers in your journal.

1. Have you ever experienced abuse in any of your relationships? If yes, describe the situation and the type of abuse you experienced.

2. When you realized you were being abused, how did it make you feel? Did you feel scared, angry, or powerless? Write down your thoughts and emotions in your journal.

3. How did you handle the situation? Did you address it with the person who was abusing you, or did you keep quiet about it? Write down your thoughts and feelings in your journal.

4. Reflect on the idea that abusive behavior can be transformed. Do you believe that this is true? Have you ever experienced or witnessed abusive behavior being transformed? Write down your thoughts and feelings in your journal.

If you are currently in an abusive relationship, seek guidance from a professional. It is important to prioritize your safety and well-being.

My Blood Runs Pink

Upon moving back in with my parents, I felt a shift in my life happen. Every major shift in my life has been over New Year's Eve, and this was no different. I was determined to start my life over and create a more positive environment for myself. I wanted a hair and makeup makeover and a life makeover! That's when I was introduced to my "Pink" relationship with a cosmetics company by a neighbor. My blood runs pink because when I was first introduced to this company, positive vibes were infused into their products and pink has always been a bright and positive color to me.

There are so many great things about this time of my life, and a lot has to do with the influence of being a part of a great organization. I didn't realize how much I was craving to be a part of a circle of women who were uplifting, positive, and encouraging. I had never had this in my life, and I started to see a transformation within myself the more I continued to be involved with the company.

As you can see in some of these before and after pictures, the before pictures show that I didn't know how to apply makeup, and I didn't feel very attractive.

After my mental health crisis in high school, I found it difficult to feel good about my appearance. I felt like my inner self was shattered, and I couldn't even begin to think about my outer appearance. To me, being beautiful seemed like a distant dream that I would never achieve, so I stopped putting any effort into it. I cut my hair short, stopped wearing makeup, and dressed in clothes that made me feel frumpy and unattractive.

But deep down, I knew something wasn't right. I didn't want to be seen or noticed by others, but I craved attention and affection. I wanted someone to tell me I was beautiful and that they loved me. This internal conflict between what I wanted and what I needed was the reason why I found myself in unhealthy relationships with men who didn't respect or value me.

Joining the cosmetics company was a turning point in my journey toward self-love and self-care. At first, I was hesitant to get involved because I still had insecurities and doubts about my appearance. But as I began to attend meetings and learn more about the beauty industry, I realized that it was more than just looking pretty. It was about feeling confident and empowered in my skin.

As I started using the beauty products, I began to experiment with different makeup looks and styles. I even started to enjoy getting ready in the morning and putting together outfits that made me feel good about myself. It was a small but important step toward reclaiming my sense of identity and self-worth.

At first, it was a struggle to break out of my frumpy and self-deprecating habits. But the more I invested in myself, the more I started to see positive changes in my mental and emotional state. I no longer felt like I needed to hide behind baggy clothes and an unkempt appearance. Instead, I began to embrace my natural beauty and unique features.

As my outer appearance began to shift, so did my inner landscape. I started to feel more confident and secure in my skin. I was no longer seeking validation from others, but instead found validation within myself. My self-esteem and self-confidence began to flourish, and I started to feel like the best version of myself.

While some may argue that true self-love and self-care come from within, my journey with a cosmetic company showed me that how we present ourselves to the world can significantly impact our self-perception. By taking care of our outer appearance, we can begin to shift our inner beliefs and transform our relationship with ourselves.

As I continued my journey of self-discovery, I realized that I had been holding myself back by fearing failure. I had been so afraid of making mistakes that I had never taken any risks or pursued my true passions. However, through my experiences in the cosmetic company, I began to learn about the importance of embracing failure as a necessary step toward success.

In addition, I learned about the power of self-love and how it can impact every aspect of life. By treating myself with kindness and compassion, I was able to shift my perspective and start seeing my worth and value.

I also discovered the importance of setting goals and working toward them with determination and perseverance. I learned to have grit in the face of obstacles and challenges and to always keep pushing forward no matter how difficult things may seem.

Another important lesson I learned was to focus on my strengths instead of constantly critiquing myself for my weaknesses. By recognizing and celebrating my unique talents and abilities, I was able to build my confidence and self-esteem.

And finally, I learned about the power of positivity and how it can inspire others and create a ripple effect of goodness in the world. By focusing on the good in myself and others, I was able to cultivate a sense of grace and gratitude that helped me find joy and fulfillment in everything I did.

Growing up in a cosmetic company was a transformative experience for me. The women who were already successful in the business became my role models and mentors, and they taught me everything I needed to know about achieving success in my own right. They showed me the importance of setting goals and working hard to achieve them, and they also taught me about the importance of good business sense.

When I started working with a cosmetic company, I was at a point in my life where I was searching for something more. I had been feeling unfulfilled in my job and my personal life and I knew that there had to be more to life than what I was currently experiencing. That's when something just clicked for me.

As I began my journey as an independent beauty consultant, I started to realize that there was so much more potential within me than I had ever realized before. I was challenged to step out of my comfort zone and try new things, and I started to see that I was capable of achieving more than I had ever imagined.

Attending the cosmetic seminars in Dallas was a turning point for me. Seeing the dancers on stage and hearing the words of encouragement from the performers filled me with a sense of energy and excitement that I had never experienced before. I felt like I was part of a community of women who were all working toward a common goal, and that was incredibly empowering.

From that moment on, I knew that this cosmetic company was more than just a business opportunity—it was a way of life. I had found a community of like-minded women who were all working toward their own goals, and I felt like I belonged. My blood started to run pink, and I knew that I had found my home.

Through my journey, I learned to believe in myself and my abilities. I learned that anything is possible with hard work, determination, and a positive attitude. And most importantly, I learned that I was capable of creating the life I wanted for myself.

As I became more involved with the company, I started to see the results of my hard work paying off. At the age of twenty-five, I became a Pink Cadillac Sales Director, becoming the youngest sales director in Virginia to be driving a Pink Cadillac, which was a huge accomplishment for me. Not only was it a symbol of my success within the company, but it was also a sign that I was able to achieve something that few other people my age had been able to accomplish.

Breaking records within my National Area was a huge achievement for me. It was a sign that my hard work and dedication to the company were paying off, and it also gave me a sense of pride and accomplishment that I had never experienced before.

Perhaps the most significant achievement I had within the company was earning an executive income within my first two years. This was something that I never thought would be possible for me, but through my hard work and dedication, I was able to achieve it. It was a sign that I had truly made it in the business world, and it also gave me a sense of financial security that I had never experienced before.

I used to believe that I needed to earn love through my achievements, which was a mindset I developed during my time with the cosmetic company. Even though it had a tremendously positive impact on my life, I still carried this belief with me. While I loved the idea of working from home and having the flexibility to eventually raise children without putting them in daycare, I realized that I was leading with the wrong intention. I was trying to prove myself instead of working toward my goals with pure intentions. Nonetheless, I worked hard every day in my business to remind myself that I was worthy of love, praise, and respect.

I still remember the day when I turned in my old Honda Civic with 200,000 miles on it and picked up a brand-new car that was free, all thanks to my hard work and dedication. As I sat in the driver's seat of my brand-new company car, I couldn't help but feel an overwhelming sense of pride and accomplishment.

But what made that moment even more special was the fact that it had silenced all the doubters and naysayers who had initially dismissed my involvement with the cosmetic company as just another fleeting hobby. I vividly recall people telling me that it was a waste of time and that I would never succeed in the business. Yet, as I started to achieve more and more milestones, even those same people began to change their tune.

It was incredible to see how my unwavering commitment to my goals started to turn their opinions around. People who had once doubted me and my abilities were saying things like, "One day she might own the company." It was a testament to the fact that hard work and persistence can truly pay off, even in the face of skepticism and doubt.

I was also pleasantly surprised to see how my involvement with the company had brought me closer to my mother. Initially, she was skeptical about the company and the products, but as she saw the positive changes in me and the way I was helping other women, she became my biggest supporter. Even today, she continues to encourage me in my endeavors and is proud of all that I have achieved.

But what made the experience special was the community I had built along the way. I met so many amazing women—fellow consultants, customers, and even my team members—and it was incredible to see the impact that we were all making together.

One of the most rewarding aspects of my work was seeing the transformations in the women I worked with. Whether it was helping them find the perfect shade of lipstick or empowering them to start their own businesses, it was an incredible feeling to know that I was making a difference in their lives. Seeing them gain confidence, feel beautiful, and achieve their own goals was truly fulfilling.

All of this fueled my passion to keep growing within the company. I wanted to continue making a positive impact and inspiring others to do the same. And as I drove off in my new car, I knew that this was only the beginning of my journey.

As my business continued to grow, I found myself spending more and more time working and less time enjoying my personal life. I would often stay up late at night working on my business, neglecting my own needs for rest. I also struggled with setting boundaries and saying no to work-related requests, even when they conflicted with important events or commitments in my personal life.

At times, I felt like I was missing out on important moments with my family and friends. I had to miss important events like birthdays, family vacations, and holidays, all because I was so focused on my business. It was difficult to balance my personal life and my work life, and I often felt like I was sacrificing one for the other.

Moreover, I also found myself becoming increasingly isolated from my loved ones. As my business grew, my social circle became mostly limited to my team and other consultants. I struggled to find time for friends who were not involved in the business and felt like I was losing touch with them.

Despite these challenges, I still loved my cosmetic journey and was grateful for the opportunities it had provided me. However, I knew that I needed to find a better balance and prioritize my well-being and personal relationships as well.

At first, it was difficult to make the necessary changes in my life. I had to confront the reality that my single-minded focus on work had caused me to neglect important aspects of my personal life. I had missed out on important events, and I had lost touch with hobbies and interests that used to bring me joy.

However as I started to make small changes, such as scheduling regular date nights with my new partner or taking time to pursue hobbies on weekends, I noticed a significant improvement in my overall well-being. I started to feel more fulfilled and happier, and my relationships with loved ones improved.

I also learned the importance of setting boundaries and being able to say no to things that weren't aligned with my values or goals. This allowed me to focus on what truly mattered and avoid burnout.

I realized that success in one area of life shouldn't come at the expense of other areas and that a balanced approach to life was essential for long-term happiness and fulfillment. This new perspective helped me to continue to grow and achieve in my career while also nurturing my relationships and self-care.

One of the greatest gifts that the cosmetic company gave me was the power of positivity. I learned how to approach challenges with a can-do attitude and to focus on the good in any situation. This mindset has helped me in all areas of my life, not just my career. I have found that when I approach life with a positive attitude, I attract more uplifting experiences and people into my life.

Another valuable lesson that I learned was resilience. Building a business is not easy, and there were times when I faced setbacks and failures. However, I learned to bounce back and keep going, even when things seemed impossible. This skill has served me well in all areas of my life, as I have faced other challenges and obstacles.

As I reflect on my cosmetic journey, I feel a sense of gratitude for all the experiences and opportunities it brought into my life. It hasn't been just a career for me, it was a way of life. I learned so much about myself and the world around me through my time with the company.

Keep in Mind

- Look for the major shifts in your life and decide to start over and create a more positive environment.
- Find ways to boost your confidence and transform your self-perception.
- As your outer appearance changes, your inner landscape shifts, and you'll start feeling more confident and secure in your skin.
- Learn about the importance of embracing failure as a necessary step toward success and the power of self-love in transforming one's life.
- Learn about setting goals, working toward them with determination and perseverance, and focusing on your strengths rather than weaknesses.
- Despite the achievements, be sure to find a balance between work and personal life.
- Acknowledge the power of positivity and resilience as well as the value of hard work.

Worksheet

1. What areas of your life need improvement?
   a. Are you satisfied with your relationships, career, health, or finances?
   b. How can you make positive changes in these areas?
2. Who are the people in your life that uplift and encourage you?
   a. Are there any relationships that are negative or draining?
   b. How can you create a more positive environment and surround yourself with people who make you feel good about yourself?
3. Do you embrace who you are, flaws and all?
   a. How can you practice self-love *and* take care of yourself?
   b. Are you too hard on yourself when things don't go as planned?
4. How do you handle failure and mistakes?
   a. Do you see them as opportunities to grow and learn?
   b. Are you willing to take risks and try new things?
5. Do you have grit and grace when facing challenges and obstacles?
   a. How can you stay persistent and committed to your goals, while also accepting setbacks and maintaining a positive attitude?
   b. Have you explored your interests and passions?

6. What brings you joy and fulfillment?

    a. How can you incorporate these activities into your daily life?

    b. How do you prioritize self-care?

7. Are you taking care of your physical, mental, and emotional well-being?

    a. What activities help you relax and recharge?

    b. Who is in your community and how do they support you?

8. Are there groups or organizations that align with your passions and values?

    a. How can you connect with people who offer encouragement, support, and advice?

    b. What truly matters to you in life?

9. How can you prioritize the things that bring you joy and fulfillment?

    a. Are success and achievement the only measures of a fulfilling life?

    b. Do you practice gratitude regularly?

10. How can you focus on the things in your life that you are grateful for?

    a. Can you make a habit of writing down three things you're grateful for each day?

Does Christ Drive a Pink Cadillac?

Growing up, my family wasn't very religious. We never went to church, but we still celebrated Christmas every year. I didn't understand the significance of the holiday other than the gifts and festive cheer. I had heard that it was a celebration of Jesus's birthday, but that didn't mean much to me.

When I was around twelve years old, I had a vivid and unsettling dream. In the dream, I was being crucified, suspended by my hands and feet, while blood dripped from the holes left in my body. It was an incredibly distressing experience, and when I woke up, I was both scared and confused.

I went to my mom and told her about the dream. She listened patiently and then gently explained to me that Jesus Christ was also crucified similarly. She encouraged me to do some research about Jesus and his struggles since I seemed to be dreaming about them.

When my mom suggested that I research Jesus, I didn't take her up on it. I was confident that I didn't need anyone else to tell me what my dream experiences meant. Little did I know that many people believed that my dream was prophetic and a sign of my spiritual awakening.

I would not see the connections until I was much older, but at least the dream had enough of an impact on my young mind to stick with me until I could understand it more.

Being a part of a cosmetic company was not just about selling makeup and earning money, it was also a pivotal moment in my spiritual journey. Through the company, I was able to meet other Christians and learn more about Jesus and the Bible. July 2002 was my Christian birthday when I accepted Jesus into my heart. This was such an important time in my spiritual development. For the first time in my life, I felt safe, not just saved. I knew that Jesus loved me and I loved Jesus.

But as a new Christian, I was still struggling to understand the concept of unconditional love and acceptance. I'd never been taught unconditional anything in my life, and the lack of a true example left me in a space of repeating patterns that didn't serve me. I believed that if I followed all the rules and did everything right, then I would be loved and accepted by God. This led me to be judgmental toward others who didn't share my beliefs or values, and I even saw myself as superior to them.

At one point in my life, I believed that God was an all-powerful, all-knowing entity that ruled over everything. I saw myself as small and insignificant in the grand scheme of things. I thought that my only purpose was to serve and obey this God, hoping to gain some favor or reward from him. I gave away my power, my agency, to this idea of an Almighty God.

When I started to feel disconnected from my inner self and the concept of inherent worth, I began to rely on external factors to earn the love and acceptance I craved. I felt like I had to do certain things, like helping women or achieve a high-ranking position, to prove my worth and gain validation from others and my newfound religion. I believed that my actions and accomplishments determined my value and whether or not I deserved love.

My perfectionism also played a role in this belief system. I thought that if I could have the perfect marriage, be obedient to authority figures, and avoid having negative thoughts, then I would be worthy of love and acceptance. This caused me to constantly strive for perfection in all areas of my life, putting a tremendous amount of pressure to achieve an unattainable standard.

In my mind, my worth was conditional on my actions and external circumstances. I was trapped in the belief that I had to earn love, rather than realizing that I was already deserving of love simply by existing.

As I became more involved in my faith and sought to earn love and approval from God, I also began to judge others who didn't meet my standards of righteousness. I convinced myself that I was doing all the right things to earn God's favor, and anyone who wasn't doing the same was simply not as good or as godly as me.

I found myself looking down on others who didn't believe in Jesus or who didn't follow the same strict religion-based moral code that I did. I would criticize their behavior and attitudes, even for the most trivial things, and felt that I was somehow superior to them.

The sad part of this way of thinking is that I was allowing outside protocols, rules, and expectations to determine whether or not I was worthy of being loved and being Christian. But as I started to question and explore my beliefs, I began to realize that this way of thinking was limiting and disempowering. I started to see that I was *not* separate from God, but rather an integral and valuable *part of the divine.* It wasn't until I discovered the soft grace of the Goddess along with the God that I was able to experience the divine daily. It was also only through Christian maturity and understanding Jesus's message of love that I realized my mistake. Jesus didn't come to judge or condemn, but to love and forgive. He integrated the female and male aspects of God perfectly because he was God and Goddess incarnate. He provided the love, healing, and nurturing of the Goddess while also giving clear instructions on how to treat others and where to put focus as an amazing masculine leader. Jesus welcomed sinners and outcasts, and his most important message was love.

That bears repeating: his most important message was *love;* you can do everything right but if you don't have love, you do *nothing* right in the eyes of God.

I learned to tap into my inner strength and wisdom, trusting my intuition and inner guidance. I started to see that I had the power to create my reality, and to shape my own life according to my desires and values. I no longer felt the need to give away my power to an external God, but instead, I embraced my divinity and saw myself as an active cocreator with the divine.

This realization has brought a sense of liberation and empowerment to my life. I now see myself as a capable individual, worthy of love and respect. I trust myself and my abilities, knowing that I have the power to create the life I want. And while I still honor and respect the idea of a divine force or God, I no longer see myself as separate from it, but rather a part of it.

Luke 7:36-50, New Century Version:

> When one of the Pharisees invited Jesus to have dinner with him, he went to the Pharisee's house and reclined at the table. A woman in that town who lived a sinful life

learned that Jesus was eating at the Pharisee's house, so she came there with an alabaster jar of perfume. As she stood behind him at his feet weeping, she began to wet his feet with her tears. Then she wiped them with her hair, kissed them, and poured perfume on them.

When the Pharisee, who had invited him, saw this, he said to himself, "If this man were a prophet, he would know who is touching him and what kind of woman she is—that she is a sinner."

Jesus answered him, "Simon, I have something to tell you."

"Tell me, teacher," he said.

"Two people owed money to a certain moneylender. One owed him five hundred denarii, and the other fifty. Neither of them had the money to pay him back, so he forgave the debts of both. Now which of them will love him more?"

Simon replied, "I suppose the one who had the bigger debt forgiven."

"You have judged correctly," Jesus said.

Then he turned toward the woman and said to Simon, "Do you see this woman? I came into your house. You did not give me any water for my feet, but she wet my feet with her tears and wiped them with her hair. You did not give me a kiss, but this woman, from the time I entered, has not stopped kissing my feet. You did not put oil on my head, but she has poured perfume on my feet. Therefore, I tell you, her many sins have been forgiven—as her great love has shown. But whoever has been forgiven little loves little."

Then Jesus said to her, "Your sins are forgiven."

The other guests began to say among themselves, "Who is this who even forgives sins?"

Jesus said to the woman, "Your faith has saved you; go in peace."

This story reminded me that it's not my job to judge or condemn or "act as God" to others. It is not my job to determine who will be saved and who will be damned, but it is to love and forgive. And as Jesus said to the woman, "Because you believed, you are saved from your sins. Go in peace." It's my belief in Jesus and his message of love that saves me, not my actions or adherence to rules. It is my job to love and to believe.

In retrospect, I am appalled by my arrogance and self-righteousness in my early days of being a Christian. I had convinced myself that I was better than others simply because I followed a certain set of rules and beliefs. I realize now that this way of thinking was harmful and unfair to those around me, and that true love and compassion require humility and an open heart toward others, regardless of their beliefs or actions.

Looking back on that experience now, I realize that it was a pivotal moment in my spiritual journey. It was the first time I thought about the idea of Jesus and what he stood for. It took me many years to come to terms with my own beliefs and to fully understand the significance of that dream, but I'm grateful for the experience and the path it set me on.

As I continue on my spiritual journey, I strive to remember this lesson and focus on loving and accepting others, regardless of our differences. And as for the question of whether Christ drives a Pink Cadillac, it's not about the car or material possessions, but about the love and message that the company represents—empowering women to be their best selves and spreading positivity and kindness.

Keep in Mind

- Becoming a part of a cosmetic company was a significant turning point in my spiritual journey.

- As a new Christian, I initially struggled with the concept of unconditional love and acceptance. I believed that I had to follow all the rules and earn God's favor to be loved and accepted.

- Feeling disconnected from my inner self, I sought validation from external factors. I believed I had to accomplish certain things and meet specific expectations to prove my worth and gain love.

- Perfectionism fueled my belief that I had to achieve an unattainable standard to be worthy of love and acceptance. This mindset put immense pressure on me.

- Questioning my beliefs, I realized that relying on external rules and expectations limited my sense of worth and disempowered me. I started to recognize my divinity and embraced the idea of being a cocreator with the divine.

- Through Christian maturity and understanding, I discovered that Jesus's most important message was love. I learned to tap into my inner strength, trust my intuition, and see myself as deserving of love and respect.

Worksheet

Being on a spiritual journey is not just about following certain beliefs or practices, but also about discovering who we truly are and our connection to the world around us. One important aspect of spirituality is understanding the concept of unconditional love and acceptance, both for ourselves and for others. In this worksheet, we will explore this theme and how we can cultivate more love and acceptance in our spiritual lives.

Section 1: Reflecting on Your Spiritual Beliefs

1. What are your current beliefs about spirituality and how they relate to love and acceptance?

2. Are there any biases or judgments you hold toward certain beliefs or practices? How can you work on letting go of these?

3. What spiritual practices or rituals do you currently engage in that help you cultivate more love and acceptance?

Section 2: Learning from Spiritual Examples

1. Think of a spiritual teacher or figure that you admire. How do they embody the qualities of unconditional love and acceptance?

2. Is there a story or parable from any spiritual tradition that resonates with you in terms of love and acceptance? What can you learn from it?

3. Reflect on a time when you felt loved and accepted unconditionally. How can you bring more of that energy into your spiritual practice?

Section 3: Practicing Unconditional Love and Acceptance

1. Identify someone in your life who you may have been judging or holding a bias toward. How can you work on seeing them with more love and acceptance?

2. Think of a situation in which you could respond with more love and acceptance, rather than judgment or criticism. What actions can you take to cultivate those qualities?

3. How can you practice self-love and acceptance in your spiritual practice? What practices or rituals can you engage in to remind yourself of your inherent worth and value?

Unconditional love and acceptance are at the core of many spiritual traditions and practices. By reflecting on our beliefs, learning from spiritual examples, and practicing love and acceptance in our daily lives, we can deepen our spiritual journeys and bring more love and positivity into the world.

Coping with PTSD in Marriage

When I met Michael, my first husband, I was at a low point in my life, right before I went into cosmetics. I had just ended a toxic relationship and moved back in with my parents, feeling lost and unsure of what to do next. Then, Michael came into my life like a shining light, offering me stability, humor, and kindness. He seemed like the perfect knight in shining armor, ready to save me from all my struggles.

We started dating soon after we met, and at first, everything seemed great. I was grateful for his support and love, and I felt like I had finally found someone who truly cared about me. But as time went on, I began to realize I had made a mistake. I had jumped into another relationship without taking the time to figure out what *I* wanted and needed in life.

Looking back, I can see now that there were some warning signs in our relationship that I chose to ignore. Michael and I had very different views on gender roles, but I convinced myself that we could make it work. I was in love, and I believed that love could conquer all. But love alone isn't enough to sustain a healthy, long-term relationship.

After we got married, Michael's desire for a traditional wife became more apparent. He didn't want me to focus on my career or business goals; he wanted me to prioritize our home and family instead. I tried to compromise, but it never felt right. I felt like I was suppressing a fundamental part of myself, and it took a toll on my mental health.

At the same time, I found myself trying to change Michael as well. I wanted him to be more supportive of my dreams and aspirations, but he couldn't understand why I was so driven. We both wanted the other person to fit into a certain mold that wasn't true to who we were as individuals.

Despite the growing tension in our relationship, I refused to give up. I was determined to make it work, even if it meant sacrificing my happiness and authenticity. Looking back, I can see how my stubbornness contributed to the breakdown of our marriage. I should have been more willing to let go and pursue what or who was truly right for me, like a man who honestly wanted kids or didn't shame me for spending money. But in the moment, it was hard to see beyond the love and security that I had initially felt with Michael.

We started therapy during our first year of marriage, attempting to fix something that wasn't broken. We were trying to change our intrinsic natures, which was impossible. I felt like a bird whose wings had been clipped and everything about me triggered him.

As time went on, the strain in our marriage continued to grow. The arguments became more frequent and intense, and the love we once shared became harder to find. I began to feel like I was living a double life, one where I had to sacrifice my ambitions and dreams to please my husband and one where I longed for the freedom to be myself and pursue my goals.

I tried to talk to Michael about our issues, but he always seemed dismissive of my concerns. He believed that his traditional views on marriage were the right way to go, and he was not willing to compromise or change his beliefs. As a result, I began to feel neglected and unimportant, like my opinions and desires didn't matter to him.

Despite this, I still clung to the relationship because of my fear of financial instability, though I was still very successful in my cosmetic business at the time. I felt like I had invested too much time and energy into the marriage to just let it go, and the idea of starting over from scratch was daunting. At the same time, Michael seemed to hold onto our marriage because of my appearance, even though we were emotionally and spiritually disconnected. When you hold onto a relationship for superficial reasons, it is destined to crumble, and that's what happened to us.

Eventually, the cracks in our relationship became too wide to ignore, and we both realized that we were holding onto a marriage that was no longer serving us. It was a painful and difficult decision, but we both knew it was time to let go and move on. We parted ways, and while it was not easy, it was the right thing to do for both of us.

During my marriage with Michael, we both created a lot of patterns that caused trauma and PTSD. I hid things from him because I was scared to face how he would act when he found out. For example, after we got married, I was not making enough money to pay the bills, and my business wasn't doing as well as it had the year before we got married.

What could have been just a minor setback turned into a major one because of our dysfunctional relationship. I would hide things for fear of his anger, and he would get mad about the hiding and then get angrier when he knew I wasn't telling the truth about hiding things from him. And so the cycle continued until we both created a financial nightmare for each other that took years to climb out of.

We also had very different ways of looking at life and business. I wanted to move forward with things because they felt right in my heart, but he wouldn't move forward with it until it logically made sense. This caused my free spirit to rebel and do things anyway even if he wasn't on board with it. I perceived his control attempts as a direct attempt to cage my heart and keep me from living out my dreams and desires.

Every time I did something that he had asked me not to, he felt disrespected and believed he didn't matter. And every time he tried to control me, I pushed back and rebelled more.

I remember fighting with Michael about money every time we brought the subject up. And so I started to put things on credit cards so that it wouldn't come out of our bank account to be noticed, and I started to move money around so that he wouldn't see how much money we didn't have. Eventually, this led to us having separate bank accounts, which was the worst thing we could do since it caused us to continue in our destructive patterns around money.

After years of living in these dysfunctional patterns, we both grew resentment around our hearts. We stopped being on the same team and started working against each other.

My marriage began to be the most painful relationship in my life instead of the best relationship in my life. We both held onto this discomfort because we didn't want to be alone. But it's just like that cliché "When it is more painful to stay where you are than it is to change, you will change." I didn't have the courage to change until years later when we had the twins, and I realized how incredibly lonely I was.

I now realize I could have made a different choice if I had been wiser. If I could go back in time and talk to my younger self, I would advise her to take a step back and focus on herself before getting into another relationship. I would encourage her to get her apartment, get the dog she always wanted, and take the time to figure out who she was and what she wanted out of life.

I now understand that relationship-hopping does not work unless you have done the inner work to address the issues that led to your previous failed relationships. I wish I had known this back then, but I am grateful for the lessons I learned along the way. Although my relationship with Michael did not work out in the end, I am grateful for the time we spent together and the lessons I learned from that experience.

To this day, I still experience intense, triggering feelings when I have something to tell my new husband that I think he won't be happy with, feeling as if he will react the same way Michael did. I have to constantly remind myself that my new husband is a different person, and I have no reason to hide anything from him to protect myself. I won't be crying for hours just because I told him something he didn't want to hear.

Our minds are incredible tools that have the power to shape our experiences and perceptions of the world. However, they can also be our worst enemy if we're not careful. When we experience something repeatedly, our mind creates patterns and habits that become familiar to us. These patterns and habits can be helpful if they are healthy and productive, but they can also be harmful if they are negative and destructive.

For example, if we grew up in a home where we were constantly criticized and put down, we may develop a negative inner voice that tells us we are not good enough. This negative self-talk can become a habit, and we may find ourselves constantly putting ourselves down even when we are successful.

Similarly, if we have a history of unhealthy relationships, we may find ourselves attracted to the same type of partner over and over again because it's what we know.

Breaking out of these patterns and habits can be difficult, but it's crucial if we want to live a happy and fulfilling life. We need to learn to recognize when our mind is leading us down a negative path and take steps to redirect it. This could involve working with a therapist or coach, practicing self-compassion and mindfulness, and intentionally seeking out new experiences and perspectives.

Ultimately, it's important to remember that we have the power to shape our minds and our lives. We can choose to break free from negative patterns and create new, healthy ones that serve us better. It's not always easy, but it is possible with effort and intention.

Emotional and mental abuse can be insidious and difficult to recognize, especially if the victim has no prior experience with it. The abuse may take various forms, such as gaslighting, manipulation, name-calling, and belittling. The abuser may use these tactics to control the victim, make them feel helpless and powerless, and ultimately, strip away their self-esteem.

The victim may find themselves in a constant state of anxiety, always on edge and walking on eggshells to avoid triggering the abuser's anger. They may begin to second-guess themselves and their perceptions of reality, doubting their intuition and judgment. Over time, the victim may lose their sense of self and become dependent on the abuser for validation and self-worth.

It can be difficult for victims of emotional and mental abuse to break out of the cycle because they often internalize the blame and feel responsible for their partner's abusive behavior. They may even feel that the abuse is somehow justified and that they deserve it. I remember thinking, *If I had been more responsible and hadn't bounced that check, my partner wouldn't have to berate me and treat me like a child.*

To break free from this cycle, it's important to recognize that the abuse is not the victim's fault and that they deserve to be treated with respect and dignity in their relationships.

In my own experience, I found that breaking out of this cycle required a lot of self-reflection and self-discovery. I had to learn to trust my feelings and intuition and to value my own needs and boundaries. This was a challenging process, as I had become so used to putting my partner's needs and desires ahead of my own that I didn't even know what my own needs were anymore.

Over time, I began to realize that healthy relationships are built on mutual respect, trust, and communication. It's important for both partners to feel valued and heard, and for both to be willing to compromise and work together to create a relationship that meets both of their needs. This requires a willingness to be vulnerable and open with one another, as well as a commitment to treating each other with kindness and compassion.

In the end, I learned that true love and connection are built on a foundation of mutual respect, trust, and empathy. When both partners are willing to honor each other's thoughts, feelings, and boundaries, and work together to create a relationship that meets both of their needs, they can create a truly magical and fulfilling partnership.

Through my experience, I also learned to identify the signs of narcissistic behavior in men, which can help detect red flags early on in a relationship. These include the following, but there may be more:

1. Talking mostly about themselves and showing a grandiose attitude.

2. Being overly obsessed with material things and how they are perceived by others.

3. Criticizing or getting upset with you when you let your guard down or don't meet their expectations.

4. Trying to impress you with superficial things at the beginning of the relationship.

5. Acting differently toward you in front of others compared to when you are alone.

6. Blaming you for things not going well.

Emotional and mental abuse is just as harmful as physical abuse, but the scars are not visible. Recognizing the signs of emotional abuse and identifying narcissistic behavior early on in a relationship can help avoid becoming a victim of abuse. It is crucial to honor our thoughts, feelings, and boundaries in any relationship to co-create a healthy and fulfilling partnership.

There is another form of abuse called financial abuse. It is a form of domestic violence where an abuser uses money as a means to control and manipulate their partner. It can happen in any type of relationship, regardless of gender, sexual orientation, or socioeconomic status.

Financial abuse can take many forms, including the following:

1. Controlling access to money: The abuser may restrict their partner's access to financial resources, including bank accounts, credit cards, and cash.

2. Withholding money: The abuser may withhold money from their partner, refusing to provide financial support for necessities such as food, shelter, and medical care.

3. Sabotaging employment: The abuser may prevent their partner from working or sabotage their partner's career by interfering with job opportunities or causing them to lose their job.

4. Running up debt: The abuser may accumulate debt in their partner's name, which can harm their credit score and make it difficult for them to access financial resources in the future.

5. Forcing financial dependence: The abuser may force their partner to be financially dependent on them by making them quit their job or preventing them from seeking employment.

6. Using money as a tool for emotional abuse: The abuser may use money to manipulate their partner's emotions, such as by threatening to withhold financial support if their partner does not comply with their demands.

It's important to note that financial abuse is often a tactic used in combination with other forms of abuse, such as emotional, verbal, and physical abuse. If you suspect that you or someone you know is experiencing financial abuse, it's important to seek help and support from a trusted friend or family member, a domestic violence hotline, or a local domestic violence shelter.

Keep in Mind

- Do not ignore the warning signs in a relationship. Establish the need for more self-reflection before committing.

- If your goal is to get into a relationship to change each other to fit your ideals, it will lead to a lack of acceptance and understanding.

- Acknowledge your flaws when it comes to relating; see what is leading to the breakdown of your relationship.

- Look at the importance of doing inner work before entering new relationships.

- Our minds have the power to shape our experiences and perceptions, but they can also create harmful patterns and habits.

- Breaking free from negative patterns is crucial for living a happy and fulfilling life, involving self-awareness, therapy, and intentional change.

- Emotional and mental abuse can be difficult to recognize, especially for victims with no prior experience.

- Various forms of emotional and mental abuse include gaslighting, manipulation, name-calling, and belittling. Abusers use these tactics to control the victim, strip away their self-esteem, and make them feel helpless and powerless.

- Victims may second-guess themselves, doubt their perceptions of reality, and lose their sense of self.

- Emotional and mental abuse can have long-lasting effects on mental health and well-being.

- It is important to recognize the signs of emotional and mental abuse and seek help for oneself or others.

- Victims often internalize the blame and feel responsible for their partner's abusive behavior.

- Breaking out of the abuse cycle requires self-reflection, self-discovery, and learning to trust one's feelings and needs.

- Healthy relationships are built on mutual respect, trust, and communication.

- Recognizing signs of narcissistic behavior early on can help identify potential red flags. Signs of narcissistic behavior include self-centeredness, obsession with material things, criticism, superficial behavior, inconsistency, and blame-shifting.

- Emotional and mental abuse is as harmful as physical abuse, but the scars are not visible.
- Financial abuse can include controlling access to money, withholding money, sabotaging employment, running up debt, forcing financial dependence, and using money for emotional abuse.
- Financial abuse often occurs in combination with other forms of abuse.

Worksheet

1. Reflect on your past relationships and identify patterns of behavior that may have contributed to their failure.

    a. Did you take the time to figure yourself out before getting into another relationship?

    b. Did you try to change your partner or compromise your values to fit their expectations?

2. Recognize and acknowledge any trauma or PTSD you may have experienced in your past relationships.

    a. What triggers these feelings?

    b. How do they affect your current relationships?

    c. Are you able to communicate your needs and feelings effectively to your partner?

3. Identify any dysfunctional patterns in your current relationship.

    a. Are you and your partner fundamentally aligned in your values and goals?

    b. Are you able to communicate and work through conflicts in a healthy way?

    c. Do you feel safe, secure, and cared for in your relationship?

4. In what ways can you improve your communication with your partner?

    a. Do you actively listen to them and express your feelings and needs clearly?

    b. Are you willing to work together to find solutions to conflicts?

5. Are you willing to be vulnerable with your partner?

    a. Have you shared your past experiences and trauma(s) with them?

    b. Do you feel comfortable being open and honest about your thoughts and feelings?

    c. How can you work on building trust and vulnerability in your relationship?

6. How do you prioritize self-care in your life?

    a. Do you engage in activities that bring you joy and practice mindfulness and relaxation techniques?

    b. Are you willing to seek professional help to take care of yourself?

    c. In what ways can you prioritize your well-being?

7. Are you open to change and grow in your relationship?

    a. Are you willing to make difficult decisions for your happiness and well-being, even if it means leaving a relationship?

    b. How can you trust yourself and have faith that you will find the love and support you deserve?

8. Have you ever felt that a partner's love for you was conditional? If so, how did this affect your self-worth and relationships?

9. Reflecting on past relationships, how have you expressed your emotions and set boundaries?

    a. What have you learned from these experiences?

10. Why is it important to honor our thoughts, feelings, and boundaries in any type of relationship?

    a. How does this contribute to a healthy dynamic between partners?

11. Have you ever witnessed emotional or mental abuse in a relationship involving someone you know?

    a. If so, how did you respond and what did you learn from the experience?

12. What steps can you take to help prevent emotional or mental abuse in your relationships or those of people you know?

13. In what ways can you help raise awareness about emotional and mental abuse and its impact on victims?

    a. What actions can you take to support those who have experienced this type of abuse?

14. Where are the dysfunctional patterns in your relationship leading to hiding and dishonesty, especially around financial matters?

Seven-Eleven Match Made in Heaven

As a young woman, I had always known that I wanted to be a mother. I had dreamed of having children who would bring joy and peace to my life. When I got married to Michael, I was certain that children were the next logical step in my life and went off my birth control right away.

Of course, I was under the impression that it would happen when it needed to happen, as well. I didn't keep track of what was happening when, but I wasn't concerned things were not happening either. Michael and I weren't in a perfect marriage and it was easier to not add another human into the mix when we couldn't even manage proper communication for an extended period before we would devolve into some sort of fight.

However, I knew children were meant for me.

After five or six years of nothing happening, I was sitting in the car chatting with one of my friends when she asked, "Well, do you actually want to have kids?"

I started bawling on the spot. I thought for sure it would have happened by then even if we weren't getting along or hadn't been keeping track of things. I wanted them, so God would provide them. That was my belief.

So, I decided to be more intentional with it. I started keeping track of things, putting them in prayers, and speaking about my desire to have children to whoever would listen. I knew they were meant for me, so I needed everyone else to know it too.

However, a couple more years passed with no children and Michael being very non-committal about children and continually telling me, "We aren't ready."

Those words from my husband were a tipping point for me and I moved out on a crisis of faith and a need to get my priorities in order. That's when I decided to go through the RCA program to become Catholic.

I had this idea that if I went through everything and became a Catholic, God would save my marriage and give me what I needed to feel fulfilled and happy. Or at least more so than I was with current circumstances.

I chose Catholicism because of the focus and devotion to Mother Mary. I thought a religion that appreciated a woman as much as the Catholics did was sure to have an appreciation for the living, everyday women of the world. I wanted this community to put as much value in me as they did in the men of the community.

Through the program, I did lots of work on myself to be a better wife to my husband because first and foremost I was determined to save my marriage. I had seen what divorce looked like while I was growing up and I wanted to maintain the stability of this relationship I had committed to. It was important to me.

So, when I was baptized, my sponsor through the church told me that I should choose something to pray for that I wanted more than anything else since I would be closer to God at that time than at any other time. Our connection would be solidified through baptism.

That night, I prayed like I never had before. "Lord, please, I want to have children. Please bring children into my life."

As I was receiving my baptism and praying for children, I heard the angels singing the word *joy* around me, "Joy! Joy! Joy!" It felt so affirming and like I was being heard by God.

Five months after my baptism, I received a divine message to move to Colorado. I hadn't lived there since college and my parents had moved back since my debacle with my ex in Florida, so my entire support system was in the mountains. There was something about being closer to them that felt necessary, so I told Michael I wanted to move.

Of course, he had just started a new job and bucked that idea immediately, but I stressed that I *needed* to move to Colorado. It was important. Finally, after tons of arguments and loads of convincing, my husband and I packed up our belongings and moved to Colorado to be closer to my parents. It was a new beginning for us, I was changing my life by what I felt God was calling me to do, and I was determined to start a family.

Just six months after we moved to Colorado, I found out I was pregnant. I blessed me with not one, but two children—Taitum and Olivia. Though Michael had been relatively non-committal to having children, he had always had a strong opinion about names and already had Taitum picked out. Then, when the girls were born, Michael also suggested the name Olivia, which I also really liked and agreed with. The names of my children carry so much meaning and significance to me. Taitum means "Bringer of Joy," and Olivia means "Bringer of Peace."

I believe that my children are my guardian angels in human form. They have brought so much joy and peace to my life, and I am grateful for every moment I have with them.

Taitum, with her infectious laughter and bubbly personality, truly lives up to her name. She brings joy to everyone around her and is always eager to share her happiness with others. Olivia, on the other hand, has a calming presence that brings a sense of peace wherever she goes. She is wise beyond her years and has a way of making everyone feel heard and understood.

As a mother, I feel so blessed to have been given these two beautiful souls to love and cherish. They have taught me so much about love, patience, and the importance of finding joy and peace in everyday moments.

When I look at Taitum and Olivia, I am reminded of the power of prayer and the blessings that come from having faith. I am grateful to God for answering my prayers and for giving me two amazing children who bring so much joy and peace to my life.

Of course, I have learned so many things as a mom. First and foremost is the ability to have patience, sometimes more patience than I've ever had in my life. I've learned how to love the imperfect and set healthy boundaries in a way that encourages my children to act in matters of choice instead of necessity or expectation or a fear of discipline. I've learned to empower my children to speak up for what they believe in and become individuals with their interests and hobbies. Of course, that has helped me practice my individuation and independence as a person outside of being a mom. And most importantly, I've learned how to give myself and my kids grace in situations I know all of us could have done better in and maybe didn't have the energy or motivation to take it all the way.

My children taught me the value of treating myself and others like humans. They continue to learn and grow and teach me things I wasn't fortunate enough to learn before they came along and that is both humbling and inspiring to me.

Self-care as a parent is so important, though. I certainly couldn't be my best for my kids if I didn't ensure I was taken care of. So, here are some ways I stay feeling capable, confident, and on top of things as a mom:

- I get enough sleep and stay hydrated.
- I plan date nights with my partner every week and set up adult-only time.
- I set up intimacy with my partner multiple times a week to balance my energy and time spent with each of my family members.
- I make a point to wear clothes that help me acknowledge various parts of my body and don't always cover up or hide parts of myself. This includes showcasing aspects of myself, like my mom tummy in a crop top, that help me feel whole and inspire me to do more healing work around self-love.

Keep in Mind

- Be more intentional and actively pursue your goals.
- Follow your intuition.
- Remember the importance of self-care as a parent and find strategies for staying capable, confident, and balanced in your role as a mom.

Worksheet

Instructions: Reflect on the following questions and write down your answers. Take your time to think about your personal experiences and how you can apply the insights from this chapter to your life as a parent.

1. How have your children taught you about love, patience, and finding joy and peace in everyday moments?

2. How do you prioritize self-growth as a parent?
   a. Do you believe that personal growth is essential for good parenting?
   b. Why or why not?

3. Reflect on your parenting journey. What challenges have you faced, and how have you overcome them?
   a. What have you learned about yourself as a parent?

4. How do you balance taking care of your children with taking care of yourself?
   a. What are some ways you practice self-care?

5. How does faith or spirituality influence your parenting style?
   a. In what ways do you teach your children about faith or spirituality?

6. How do you instill values of joy and peace in your children's lives?
   a. What are some practical ways you encourage them to live a joyful and peaceful life?

7. What are some ways you can continue to grow and evolve as a parent?
   a. How can you prioritize personal growth while raising children?

8. How can you ensure that you are being present in the moment and savoring the time you have with your children, even during challenging moments?

    a. What are some mindfulness practices that you can incorporate into your daily life as a parent?

Remember, parenthood is a journey that requires constant self-reflection and growth. Use the insights from this chapter to deepen your awareness of yourself as a parent and to continue to evolve and grow in your role.

The Unveiling Begins with Nita Marie

After nearly two decades of trying to make things work with Michael, I finally asked for a divorce. I knew if I didn't start making changes I would end up becoming a resentful old woman. Asking for the divorce kickstarted many things in my life.

Once the divorce was moving, Michael decided to stop providing financial support, and that put the girls and me further into debt. I was completely broke, in debt, and qualified for food stamps. One day, I remember scrambling quarters together to get groceries for the girls, and I knew at that moment something needed to change. That was when I had the divine idea to start modeling again.

When I was in college, I did some nude modeling for the art and photography classes. I loved it, especially the positive attention it brought, but I did not have the strength and boundaries necessary to ward off the negative attention. There were a few people who would say creepy or uncomfortable things to me or about me, and I did not have the wherewithal to stop them. So, I allowed our interactions to trickle away and that eventually led me to stop modeling just so I could avoid them.

The new form of modeling I wanted to do was not for money at first. I always felt most alive and confident when I received attention, even sexually. So, after all of the difficult things in my life happening, I wanted to give myself a boost to get back out there.

I had a friend who was a new photographer and we started talking about her goals and about what I was planning on doing with modeling. My friend suggested that we help each other out where she took photos of me for free and then we could both use those photos for business purposes. Considering I was still financially down after the divorce, I couldn't have asked for a better opportunity.

So, I headed to her makeshift studio space and stripped down to lingerie for a boudoir photoshoot. The images were beautiful and made me feel sensual, beautiful, sexy, and empowered.

I was deeply inspired after that shoot. The photos my friend took looked so good and made me feel so beautiful and confident that I couldn't help but share some of them on Facebook. I wouldn't recommend doing that now as I think it's important to keep your business and personal lives separate, especially when it comes to more mature and risqué business endeavors, but I had been struggling for so long that having something positive come along was worth sharing to my loved ones.

As I shared these photos on Facebook, I realized the power of embracing my body and sexuality. However, it wasn't without its difficulties, as I faced backlash from conservative friends and family. Despite the criticism, I chose to stand by my decision and reclaim ownership of my body and desires.

Although I was blossoming and rediscovering my sexuality, this transformation was met with resistance from some people around me. Coworkers reported me, claiming I was being a bad leader and setting a poor example for my unit. Christian friends removed me from leadership positions, believing that expressing myself sexually conflicted with being a Christian leader. On Facebook, some people unfriended me, and others gossiped behind my back, accusing me of selling my soul to the devil.

Amid these challenges, I found myself questioning my path. I wondered why so many of my Christian friends turned their backs on me when I believed I was following a calling. Seeking guidance, I prayed to God and received a resolute *yes* to continue in the direction I felt led. He showed me the image of Joan of Arc, who also faced disbelief and persecution despite receiving messages from God. He assured me that I, too, might be persecuted, but He would carry me through it, for He had a plan for me.

Amid losing some friends, I also gained others. While some were put off by my photos, many others were inspired by them. Women reached out to me expressing their desire to take pictures like mine. My fan base started growing, and I gained a strong following on Facebook.

Through modeling, I started getting lots of positive feedback from men. It felt really good since it had been so long since I had received much of anything positive from Michael, so men being nice and affirming to me was a positive change.

Through modeling, I ended up connecting with a group of women who also did boudoir photos and were setting up to make a calendar full of sexy photos. So, I agreed to participate and we ended up being invited to events and openings as calendar girl eye candy for the crowds and audiences.

All of the events and gigs we were invited to led to more exposure for me, so I decided to do a calendar shoot on my own. One of them was styled boudoir like the calendars I'd been doing with the group of calendar girls, and the other I decided to do topless.

Ironically, the topless version got a lot of negative feedback from the women in my life, even my other modeling friends, because they thought I was sexualizing myself. I didn't understand why they could have lingerie on and not be sexualizing themselves, but my topless photos were too much. Regardless, that stunt, albeit a financially sound and lucrative decision, also lost me some people who I thought were my friends and connections due to unnecessary judgments.

After that, because of the success of the calendars and my growing fame on Facebook, I decided to start a website where my customers could come and feel safe purchasing more explicit content and materials from me.

To generate income, I explored ways to monetize my modeling, leading to the promotion of topless calendars on Facebook and the creation of my website for exclusive content. This endeavor began to help me pay my bills and chip away at credit card debt, bringing my finances closer to matching my pervious income.

Yet, Goddess had a different plan in store. My website was shut down due to the payment processing system's restrictions on adult content. So, I thought, *Oh, great. Now what am I going to do?* This setback led me to discover Only Fans, a subscription-based website that allows adult content creators to set their prices and offer exclusive content. Though I initially joined Only Fans reluctantly, I now see that it was all part of a larger plan, especially given the impact of COVID-19 on the platform.

With my current husband's unwavering support and smart business advice, I began building my Only Fans page. Despite the initial challenges of moving in together, we committed to working through the ups and downs of our relationship. With his help and my hard work, my fan base and income rapidly grew, reaching an astonishing $40,000 per month within just six months of starting Only Fans. This level of success was beyond my wildest dreams, allowing me to pay off most of my debt and build savings. No longer did I worry about financial uncertainties or whether my debit card would go through. Within six months of starting Only Fans, I was able to pay off over $100,000 of credit card debt and put money into savings.

Three months after the events described, the COVID-19 pandemic struck America, causing an unforeseen shift in American culture. Quarantine measures confined people to their homes, leading to restrictions on work, socialization, and entertainment. During this time, the internet became a vital source of connection and amusement, setting the stage for Only Fans to explode in popularity.

Indeed, it was an explosion. Only Fans' user base skyrocketed from 900,000 in 2019 to an astounding 210 million by 2023. The number of creators on the platform surged from 100,000 to over two million during the same period. Notably, my income also experienced a meteoric rise, jumping from $45,000 per month to a staggering $180,000 per month just four months later. I was immensely grateful that I had followed God's inspiration and had not let the skeptics deter me from pursuing my calling.

I finally felt financially secure and fulfilled by what I was doing. It was as if I had become one of the most successful entrepreneurs out there, and I was genuinely enjoying my journey.

Keep in Mind

- Positive attention from men and the boost in self-confidence through modeling provided a contrast to my previous experiences with my first marriage.
- Just because some people don't approve of your choices doesn't mean they should stop you from doing anything.
- Sometimes the path forward is unexpected, but that doesn't mean you shouldn't explore it.

Worksheet

1. Has a difficult situation ever prompted you to step out and take a risk?

2. What were some of the challenges you faced in the wake of your new freedom?

3. What lessons did you learn from the experiences?

4. Have you ever pursued something new to give yourself a boost after a difficult time in your life? How did it turn out?

5. Have you ever experienced positive and negative attention for something you shared on social media? How did you handle it?

6. What is one thing you can do today to support yourself through a difficult time in your life?

7. What is some advice you would give someone else who is feeling like they need a boost after experiencing something difficult?

Sex Matters

God inspired me to be an Only Fans model.

Of course, that's not what I planned for my life, but who am I to go against God? I see now that it wasn't that he was inspiring me to be an Only Fans Model necessarily, but that Only Fans would be the vehicle in which He would help me become in tune with my sexuality and my body again.

If you believe your relationship with the three-letter word sex doesn't matter, you might be mistaken.

In truth, your connection with sex significantly impacts your ability to manifest. Creative energy and sexual energy are intertwined; they both stem from kundalini energy rising from the Earth up the spine, although they may manifest differently in individuals' lives.

People with high sex drives often tend to be highly creative, and vice versa. Unfortunately, our current American society under-values creativity as a means of achievement and survival. As a result, many highly creative individuals suppress their creativity, causing it to manifest in their sexuality. If creativity were nurtured and encouraged from a young age, most people would find equal fulfillment in creating art, music, gardens, cars, homes, and even their dream lives, as they do in engaging in sexual activities.

Misguided creativity finding expression through sex is as common as women hyper-focusing on everything else *but* sex to suppress their sexuality. This was me ten years ago; I kept myself excessively busy to avoid feeling the lack of physical touch and sexual desire I experienced after my divorce.

However, through exploration, I discovered the following transformative aspects of my sexuality:

- I transitioned from considering masturbation as gross, perverted, and wrong, to embracing the natural need for sexual release and discovering what truly turns me on.
- I shifted my focus from putting everything else before my sex life to prioritizing intimate moments with my partner, making sure we engaged in sexual activities several times per week, including him helping me achieve orgasm.
- I moved from keeping my sexual desires hidden away in a closet to openly acknowledging some of my sexual fantasies.

On the next pages, I will share some tools that have been instrumental in my journey of growth and transformation in these areas.

Masturbation Matters: Embracing Sexual Expression

Masturbation is a natural aspect of human sexuality, and it's time to open up the conversation about it, especially for women. Just like going to the bathroom daily, sexual release is a normal bodily function for both men and women. However, society has often made men feel less shameful about it, while women have been led to believe it's not appropriate to discuss or engage in it.

Most men are biologically wired to experience a sexual release regularly due to hormonal factors. This is nature's way of ensuring the human race's survival. Even if a man is not in a sexually active relationship, he still needs to release semen to relax. Suppressing this natural need could lead to unnecessary tension and frustration. Instead, we should embrace the release of oxytocin through sexual activity as a means of promoting relaxation and emotional well-being in men.

It's crucial to acknowledge that sexual thoughts and desires are a natural part of human nature. Men may secretly find women attractive and fantasize about them; it's a reality that we cannot change. While we should respect individual boundaries and consent, trying to suppress these instincts may not be the most constructive approach.

As women, it's time to reconsider the perspectives and beliefs imposed upon us. Embracing our sexuality and understanding our role in human reproduction is empowering. There's no reason to feel ashamed of expressing our desires and embracing our sensuality. Someone once mentioned to me that she believed God intended sex to just be for procreation. If that were the case, why would he/she have created women with a clitoris whose only purpose is to experience pleasure?

I believe God/Goddess wants us to experience the divine through our pleasure centers, particularly through the clitoris. Man grows closer to God as He gives the woman pleasure and women grow closer to God experiencing the pleasure. This has been my experience anyway.

Moving forward, let's recognize that God's plans may not always align with our agendas. Embracing the mysterious path She lays out for us can lead to more positive outcomes, even if there may be unexpected healing and challenges along the way.

Let's break free from the chains of shame and embrace our sexuality with confidence and self-love. It's time to foster open conversations, understanding, and acceptance surrounding the topic of masturbation and sexual expression.

Receiving God's Healing Through Adult Work

I have witnessed a direct impact on my finances by staying steady and following God's guidance, but I've also come to understand that money is not the only reward for listening to God's voice. Often, the true payoff lies in experiencing profound healing in areas where we've been stuck, forging meaningful lifelong relationships, and breaking free from ancestral trauma bonds. This kind of payoff may not always be tangible; it can be elusive and challenging to grasp. However, its rewards are far more fulfilling than mere monetary gain. While money may address many day-to-day challenges, it cannot resolve internal struggles or deepen our faith in God. It is through faith that our needs are truly provided, not the other way around, as in "I will get everything I need and then I will have faith."

Reflecting on the past five years as an adult model, I realize that both my career choice and my commitment to healing have played significant roles in my exponential personal growth. The journey of sexual healing I embarked on as an adult model and the fears I faced in my career were transformative experiences. Nevertheless, it was my conscious decision to heal that allowed me to navigate those situations and emerge healed and not bitter. I owe a great deal of gratitude to my two strong mentors who guided me through these transformations.

In my quest for personal growth, I came to a powerful realization that every challenging situation presented a choice: to grow and evolve or to become a victim and harbor bitterness. Recognizing that I always had a choice became an empowering revelation along my path.

Returning to the concept of the "Big O" (orgasms in every area of life), I've described how breaking through mental, spiritual, and energetic roadblocks creates space for God to work within us. It's akin to experiencing God orgasms, opportunities for divine intervention to inspire creativity and love, bringing joy, playfulness, and fun into our lives. I've learned to embrace this orgasmic feeling not just in my bedroom but throughout my life, releasing the need for control and allowing divine energy to flow.

Throughout this book, the provided worksheets may have triggered transformative shifts within you. If you find the process uncomfortable, you're likely on the right path. Change often occurs in the uncomfortable spaces, and the more discomfort you embrace, the greater the potential for change. However, I encourage you not to stop halfway through the process, leaving yourself unsatisfied and in pain like having "blue balls." Fully embrace the transformation and seek guidance from a reliable mentor to support you along the journey. I've listed several mentors at the back of this book for your reference. I believe that this book is just scratching the surface of areas of your life that you may want to start uncovering; your relationship with sex and your body is something that is continually changing and evolving, and I hope this book has inspired you to at least start the journey of finding what feels right to you.

Sex and Intimacy

Only Fans can be an empowering platform for women to explore their sexuality and heal past traumas if approached with the right mindset. It offers a unique opportunity to embrace diverse body types and recognize the attractiveness in all shapes. Through my coaching program, women can connect with like-minded individuals in a sex-positive and supportive community. If you're interested in starting your Only Fans page and want to learn more, visit me at www.nitamariecoach ing.com.

Sex and intimacy are fundamental human needs that have been stifled for too long in American culture. As a highly sexed individual from an early age, I used to carry shame and guilt for my desires, thinking they were wrong. Even after becoming a Christian, I attempted to suppress these feelings, but the repression found its way out in other aspects of my life, leading to anxiety, disconnection from creativity, and a sense of emptiness.

Rediscovering and embracing my sexuality was transformative. I realized that by accepting my desires and embracing intimacy, I could finally find peace, connect with my authentic self, and flow with the natural order of life. I no longer felt the need to control everything around me but instead allowed myself to experience the joy of healthy sex combined with intimacy.

To me, intimacy means sharing a deep personal connection with someone who loves your entire self, including the secret parts of you. It's about being transparent, authentic, and safe in the presence of another person. Combining intimacy with orgasms can be mind-blowing and life-changing, raising one's vibrational energy to new heights.

Consistent orgasms have numerous health benefits for the body, such as improved mental clarity, skin health, sleep quality, reduced PMS symptoms, enhanced mood, strengthened immunity, and pain relief. These advantages make it logical for women to seek daily orgasms throughout their lives. Moreover, we should educate preteens and teens about the value of masturbation to fulfill sexual needs healthily and avoid entering relationships solely for this purpose.

Promoting open conversations about sex within families can help dispel secrecy and repression, fostering a healthier understanding of sexuality. By normalizing discussions about sex, we can celebrate this natural aspect of life without perverting its essence.

Embracing our sexuality, nurturing intimacy, and experiencing healthy orgasms can truly transform our lives, enriching our mental, emotional, and physical well-being. It's time to liberate these fundamental aspects of human existence from the shadows and embrace them as essential components of a fulfilled life.

Awaken Your Clit, Awaken Your Soul

I firmly believe that awakening the clitoris is a profound way to connect with a woman's soul, her authentic self, and her pleasure center. My journey to self-discovery and self-love began when I fell in love with my clitoris. Deep within its folds lie powerful emotions, erotic pleasure, intuition, and spiritual connection. However, it may also hold sexual, emotional, and spiritual trauma from past experiences or even past lives. Ignoring and forgetting about the clit denies us the gift that God bestowed upon women—an opportunity to connect with the divine in an orgasmic way and to release pain and suffering.

The clitoris is a remarkable part of the female body, containing thousands more nerve endings than the male penis. Its sole purpose is to create pleasure, making it a unique gift that brings joy and delight to women. Sadly, this gift is often overlooked and rarely celebrated in mainstream conversations.

The question arises: why aren't more women experiencing orgasms? Studies reveal that only 20 percent of women have orgasms during sex, with 80 percent relying on masturbation to achieve climax. However, out of that 80 percent, 60 percent feel guilty about self-pleasure, preventing them from experiencing the full potential of their sexuality. Furthermore, a staggering 10-15 percent of women have never experienced an orgasm in their *entire* lives. This means that a significant portion of the female population is missing out on incredible physical, mental, and spiritual benefits that come with embracing their clitoris.

Awakening the clit is the first step in lifting the veil that has been forced upon women for too long. For me, it was the key to revealing my authentic self and embracing the divine connection within. By exploring and understanding this powerful part of ourselves, we can embark on a journey of self-discovery, empowerment, and fulfillment. Let us celebrate and honor this beautiful gift that lies within each of us, ready to awaken our souls and enrich our lives with divine pleasure and profound self-love.

For more information on how to awaken the clitoris, there is information in the following chapter worksheet.

Sex Addiction and Porn

Sexuality is a fundamental aspect of human nature, and pornography, like many things, can have both positive and negative effects on our lives. The key lies in our intentions and how we approach these aspects of our sexuality. Let's explore this further to understand how we can cultivate a healthy and fulfilling relationship with our sexuality.

Just as with alcohol or food, our intentions play a crucial role in how we experience sexuality and pornography. Enjoying a drink or a dessert occasionally can be pleasurable, but when used excessively or as an escape, it can become harmful. Similarly, sex is a natural human need, and God designed us with the desire to not only procreate but to also enjoy sexual pleasure. The clitoris itself stands as a testament to the beauty of sexual pleasure for its own sake.

Shaming natural human needs, including sexuality, can lead to an unhealthy society. Just as we normalize eating and going to the bathroom, we should strive to normalize and understand our sexual needs without judgment. Healthily embracing sexuality helps foster emotional well-being and intimate connections.

Pornography, in moderation and with intimacy, can add to the experience of sexuality and relationships. The issue arises when it becomes an addictive escape from intimacy and emotional connection. Addressing pornography addiction requires seeking help to realign sexual needs and understand the underlying reasons driving the addiction.

Emphasizing intimacy in our relationships can profoundly impact how we approach sexuality. A woman who embraces her sexuality can help guide her partner's desires toward a deeper and more connected experience. Watching porn together with intimacy and open communication can lead to shared pleasure and understanding of each other's desires.

Consent is also a large piece of a healthy sexual society. When sex is nonconsensual for either party, it can become abuse. When dealing with minors under eighteen it is important to remember that any sexual act with a minor is immoral and nonconsensual as they do not have the presence of mind to agree or disagree with the sexual act. When this happens, a huge breach of trust is broken. Because the sexual organs are the most sensitive organ in the body and I believe the gateway to the soul's emotion, having a nonconsensual sexual act done to you can create immense harm. It can create even greater harm when done by a family member or person you trust, as it is often confusing for the victim because they do not want to hurt the other person by speaking out. If you have experienced any kind of sexual abuse or molestation, I encourage you to seek professional help because *not* sharing about this pain is causing other harmful things in your life including the lack of ability to create the things you deeply desire because the sexual organs are related to creativity and desire.

As a sex worker for several years one of the biggest misconceptions about sex workers is that they have loose boundaries and will have sex with anyone to get money. This is far from the truth unless you are in a sex trafficking situation where you are being forced to have sex or to perform sex acts against your will, being in the sex work community is very much about respecting another performer's sexual boundaries and being safe. Because we talk so openly about sex, it is easy to create boundaries and to share what is comfortable and what is not when working with another performer. If a performer crosses those sexual boundaries created between performers they are often blacklisted within the community and his/her name is known as someone to not work with. There is also consistent testing done before scenes to ensure STDs are not passed among performers. With the prevalence of STDs in the college community as well as the cases of date rape and sexual assault among women in their twenties, if all men were upheld to the standards that adult creators are held to, I believe that the rise of STDs and date rape would drastically be reduced. Many women who are date raped very rarely talk about their experience for fear of being accused of provoking it or for fear of causing drama in social circles. In the sex work community, it is very normal to be called out for crossing sexual boundaries and other sex workers support each other if it happens. Being in the sex work community has helped me create a clearer image of my boundaries and my own needs sexually.

Sexuality is a beautiful and natural part of being human, and it is essential to approach it with respect, balance, and understanding. By acknowledging and embracing our sexual needs, we can cultivate healthier and more fulfilling relationships with ourselves and our partners. Remember that seeking professional help when needed can lead to transformative changes and a more aligned sexual journey.

Keep in Mind

- Your body is a unique and beautiful creation. Embrace it with love and acceptance, recognizing that your desires are natural and valid.

- While your journey may face criticism, stay committed to your path. Remember, you're not alone in facing resistance, and your personal growth is worth any challenges.

- Maintain boundaries between personal and business endeavors, especially in more mature contexts. Balance self-expression with professionalism to protect your reputation.

- Reject shame surrounding sexuality and self-expression. Shame can hinder personal growth; instead, focus on fostering a healthy relationship with your desires.

- When faced with doubt, turn inward for guidance. Seek moments of reflection and connect with your inner self through meditation, prayer, or journaling.

- As you evolve, some relationships may shift. Embrace the new connections that align with your journey and empower you to express your authentic self.

- If financial difficulties arise, explore creative solutions to overcome them. Remember, setbacks can lead to new opportunities for growth and success.

- Life is full of unexpected twists. Stay adaptable and open-minded, ready to seize new opportunities even when faced with unforeseen challenges.

- Acknowledge your progress and celebrate your accomplishments, no matter how small. Your journey is a testament to your strength and resilience.

- Alongside your pursuits, prioritize self-care. Nurture your physical, emotional, and mental well-being through activities that bring you joy and relaxation.

- Foster open conversations about sex, intimacy, and self-love. By sharing your experiences, you can contribute to a more accepting and understanding society.

- Regularly reconnect with your inner self. Engage in practices that help you tap into your intuition, creativity, and authenticity.

- Embrace personal growth, even when it challenges your comfort zone. Remember that change is often a sign of progress and a step toward self-realization.

- Your journey of self-discovery is a celebration of your sexuality and identity. Embrace your power, desires, and the profound connection they bring.

- Trust that you are exactly where you need to be on your journey. Embrace the uncertainty and trust that the path you're on will lead you to greater self-awareness and fulfillment.

Worksheet

Section 1: Reflect on Your Current Relationship with Your Pleasure

1. Take a moment to reflect on your recent experiences with orgasms.

    a. When was the last time you had an orgasm?

2. Can you recall what led to that orgasm and how you felt afterward?

    a. Consider the type of orgasms you've experienced.

    b. Have you had a vaginal orgasm or a clitoral orgasm, or both?

Section 2: Embrace Your Body

1. Body Exploration:

    a. Find a comfortable and private space where you can sit with a mirror.

    b. Take a few deep breaths to relax, then gently spread open the labium that leads to your vagina with the mirror to see your clitoris.

    c. Allow any feelings or emotions that arise to be acknowledged without judgment.

    d. Take some time to journal about your experience and how you feel after looking at your clit.

2. Love Massages:

    a. Embrace self-love and body positivity by incorporating daily or every other day love massages for your clitoris and vagina.

    b. These massages should be a gentle and loving exploration of your body, with no pressure to reach an orgasm.

   c. Use your fingers to move in circular motions around your vagina and inside it, while also gently rubbing your clitoris.

   d. Pay attention to how this practice makes you feel physically and emotionally.

Section 3: Introducing Pleasure Tools

3. Invest in a Portable Vibrator:

   a. Consider purchasing a good quality portable vibrator, which you can find online or at a sex store.

   b. Incorporate the use of your vibrator a few times a week to give yourself pleasure and experience orgasms.

4. Nipple Play:

   a. During your clitoris massages or vibrator sessions, explore nipple play and allow your mind to wander to fantasies that bring you pleasure.

Section 4: Journal Your Transformation

5. Start a Pleasure Journal:

   a. Create a dedicated journal to document your experiences and feelings throughout this journey.

   b. Note any changes you observe in your body, mental health, and overall well-being after incorporating these practices.

Remember that this journey is uniquely yours. Trust your instincts, listen to your body, and be open to exploring new depths of pleasure and self-discovery. As you awaken your clit and build a new relationship with your body, embrace the transformative power of pleasure in all its forms. Embody self-love and acceptance, knowing that you deserve to experience joy and fulfillment in your life.

The Unveiled

The butterfly has emerged as I have become unveiled. Before Only Fans, I had been living in survival mode, where every bit of money went to the essentials. Once I left survival mode, I could pay attention to myself. I believe people who get stuck in a space of necessity and survival have little room to dream and create and it limits them to such a small, narrow mindset. At least, that's how I felt when I was in the thick of things.

Thriving for me meant I could start building. It was no longer about keeping my head above water and food on the table for myself and my kids, it was about opening the doors to possibilities and showcasing all of the amazing ideas I had and could contribute to my family and my community. Being in a space where I no longer had to worry about money was the turning point.

As I made money, I realized there was a side of me that I hadn't allowed to exist in the open before. I was able to direct more of my attention to growth and healing past trauma so I could break the cycles and patterns that had brought me to debt in the first place. There was this vulnerable aspect of me who desperately wanted to take my knowledge and experiences and bring them out to the world to help others, as well.

I turned my sights on feminine advocacy. I knew when I was at my lowest, it took so much and so many people helping me for me to get to a point where I didn't feel like I was drowning, so the least I could do was give back in some way.

I recognized what attracted me to the cosmetic company was the bonding that happened with the women in the community and how much I enjoyed having these people around to help me and guide me and how much I could use my knowledge and experience to help others, but the thing that turned me off is that those relationships only existed within the bubble of the company, and the moment I stepped outside of that bubble to express that sexual side, I was discarded. I wanted something I could carry with me everywhere and bonds with women who were looking for the same. That type of relationship was hugely important to me.

As I continued to follow the threads of bonding and relationship building, I realized many people held the masculine mindset that if something wasn't of visible monetary or business value, it wasn't worth their time. They were willing to gather and attend events if it helped them build businesses and projects, but nothing beyond that.

I wondered why people couldn't appreciate time with each other in a way that had everything to do with interpersonal relationships and rest and nothing to do with making their next dollar.

So, I set out to build a space for women where they could gather without any expectations and would be able to release the stressors of life for a little. I needed that for myself, so it was only logical that others would need it too.

It was time to start honoring the women unveiled, starting with me.

I realized I felt best and most confident with fewer clothes on, or at least clothes that flattered my body. If I wear baggy clothes, I feel deeply disconnected from my body and am left completely disconnected from myself, and I want to take my whole self everywhere I go. I couldn't do life without my body. So, here are some of my tips on looking and feeling great at any age:

As mentioned before, life is so much harder without adequate sleep and hydration. Many women diminish their sex drive by not drinking enough water in a day.

I am a huge advocate for consistent orgasms. They are proven to be like a fountain of youth for women as they help move blood flow to the skin giving a more youthful appearance and helping fight breakouts. Orgasm helps with collagen production and brain functions. It aids in the production of oxytocin and dopamine, which can boost the mood. There are loads of benefits and I cannot recommend them enough.

Spend more time outside and in nature. Even if it's a quick walk around the neighborhood, it is worth it to breathe some fresh air and touch the grass if you can.

Schedule time to unplug so you can take a breath and not have to worry about anything for a little while. Being able to step back and not have to stress about anything helps me refocus. Plus, stress is the number one cause of aging signs in a person, so the more you can give yourself a break, the more youthful you'll stay!

Exercise, of course, is huge. The more we keep our bodies moving, the longer we'll be able to keep them moving into the future.

Meditate and take time to hear the inner voice that almost always leads you in the direction of your highest self. Integrating meditation into your daily practice can be like brushing your teeth for the soul and helps in keeping the veil lifted. The more a woman meditates, the clearer she becomes in the direction her soul wants to lead her, instead of feeling like she needs to mask her authentic self to exist.

Energy work is also important. I am a Reiki master and have enjoyed the benefits of energy healing for over thirty years. I started getting into breathwork when I was thirteen years old because my mom was involved in some of the alternative healing modalities. I noticed as I was learning it and growing my practice that I could feel when I was misaligned energetically and when I was right on track. I use Reiki mostly on myself and my family as I find it's a good way to recharge and get myself back up to speed with things and it helps my kids to calm down when they feel rambunctious or off-kilter.

In Reiki, a practitioner uses their hands to channel energy to the recipient, either by placing their hands on or near the recipient's body. The idea is that this energy can help to balance the recipient's energy and promote healing on physical, emotional, and spiritual levels.

Many different forms of energetic healing are practiced around the world. Some of the most common ones include acupuncture, qigong, tai chi, yoga, breathwork, and sound healing. Acupuncture involves the insertion of fine needles into specific points on the body to stimulate the flow of energy. Qigong and tai chi are Chinese practices that involve slow movements, breathing techniques, and meditation to balance and cultivate energy in the body. Yoga also incorporates physical postures, breathing, and meditation to help promote wellness and balance. Breathwork involves using different techniques to control and regulate the breath, which can have a profound effect on the mind and body. Finally, sound healing uses various instruments and techniques to create sounds and vibrations that are believed to help balance and harmonize the body's energy. Each of these practices has its unique benefits and can be used to support overall health and well-being.

As you reveal yourself and unveil yourself, you uncover your highest and best self. When we are born and come into our bodies, we already understand what our highest selves look like and it is only through the teachings and conditioning of life that we lose the vision and accessibility of our highest selves. Our goals through this work are to uncover the parts of us we buried beneath the veil and get back in touch with the loving and authentic aspects of us that continually keep us growing and improving.

The difference between like and love is depth and connection to authenticity. I was able to access love outside of myself in a healthy and secure relationship when I did the work and gave myself permission to be vulnerable and show up as the person I was born to be.

It is easy to like things and people and ourselves, but it is something more to love all of those, including ourselves. Keeping the veil lifted is part of a continued practice that will continue throughout most of your life; it's not something that you do once and it stays. I am so grateful that I was able to become aware of how the veil had become like a tomb over my life. Through God and Goddess's love and faithfulness to me, continuing to stay in touch with my own body and sexuality as well as remaining aware of what might set my veil in motion, I hope to continue to remain unveiled and to help other women have the courage to do the same. The butterfly is a beautiful sacred part of every woman that I know you deserve to see.

Keep in Mind

- Notice how being stuck in a space of necessity and survival limits one's ability to dream and create.

- Recognize the importance of opening doors to personal growth, healing past trauma, and contributing to your family and community.

- Observe how many people primarily value relationships and activities that are directly tied to monetary or business gains. Question the lack of appreciation for interpersonal connections and non-monetized aspects of life, such as rest and quality time with others.

- Feeling confident and authentic requires embracing your body and presenting yourself in a way that makes you feel connected and aligned.

- Having achieved success in online modeling, I transitioned into coaching to help others maximize their earning potential. Look at the benefits of learning from the mistakes and experiences of a seasoned professional to fast-track business growth and maintain long-term success.

- Uncover your true, authentic self and reconnect with the aspects that have been buried beneath societal conditioning. Emphasize the importance of embracing vulnerability and authenticity as a pathway to self-love and deeper connections with others.

- Accessing love outside of oneself becomes possible through personal growth, vulnerability, and showing up as your true self.

Worksheet

Chapter 15 explores the journey of self-discovery and personal growth after growing past survival mode. Use this worksheet to reflect on the key insights and apply them to your own life.

1. Self-Reflection:

    a. Take a moment to reflect on a time when you felt stuck in survival mode. How did it limit your mind-set and prevent you from dreaming and creating? What were some small steps you could take to break free from this mindset?

2. Building Possibilities:

    a. Imagine a life where you no longer have to worry about money. How would you open doors to possibilities and showcase your ideas to your family and community? List three specific ways you could contribute and make a difference.

3. Giving Back:

    a. Consider a cause or area where you feel passionate about making a positive impact. How can you give back and help others in this area? Brainstorm at least two actions you can take to contribute and support others.

4. Interpersonal Relationships:

    a. Reflect on the relationships in your life. Do you prioritize connections solely based on business or monetary value? How can you appreciate and cultivate relationships focused on interpersonal growth, rest, and support? List two ways you can enhance your relationships beyond business-oriented goals.

5. Body Acceptance and Self-Care:
   a. Explore your relationship with your body and self-image. How does your choice of clothing impact your connection to your body and sense of self? Identify ways you can dress in a manner that makes you feel confident and connected to your body.

6. Holistic Well-being:
   a. Consider the importance of sleep, hydration, and consistent orgasms in your overall well-being. Reflect on your current habits in these areas and identify one step you can take to improve each aspect (e.g., establish a regular sleep schedule, increase water intake, prioritize self-care, and explore the benefits of orgasms).

7. Nature and Unplugging:
   a. Reflect on your relationship with nature and unplug from technology. How often do you spend time outside and unplug from devices? Identify one specific activity or practice you can incorporate into your routine to spend more time in nature and unplug regularly.

8. Exercise and Movement:
   a. Evaluate your current level of physical activity. Are you keeping your body moving regularly? Identify one form of exercise or movement you enjoy or would like to explore. Create a simple plan to incorporate it into your routine.

9. Energetic Healing:
   a. Consider different forms of energetic healing (e.g., Reiki, acupuncture, yoga, breathwork). Reflect on

your interest and openness to these practices. Research and choose one form of energetic healing that resonates with you. Explore resources or practitioners in your area to begin incorporating them into your self-care routine.

10. Online Modeling and Personal Branding:

    a. Explore your interest in online modeling or personal branding. Reflect on the author's advice and tips for success. If this aligns with your goals, consider how you can treat it as a business and create content for different audience levels. Identify one action step you can take to start building your brand or online presence.

11. Seeking Guidance and Expertise:

    a. Reflect on the benefits of seeking guidance from a coach or expert in your field. Consider areas in your life or goals where professional guidance could accelerate your progress. Identify one specific area where you could benefit from coaching or mentorship and explore resources or potential experts in that field.

12. Unveiling Your Authentic Self:

    a. Reflect on the idea of uncovering your highest and best self. Consider the aspects of yourself that you may have buried beneath conditioning and societal expectations. Identify one action step you can take to reconnect.

Meditations and Rituals

We are taught how to take care of our physical health; we are starting to learn how to take care of our emotional and mental health but very few times are we taught how to take care of our ethereal health (the energy that radiates around us and within us). I hope that teachers, parents, and guardians will start to teach children how to take care of their ethereal health as much as their physical, emotional, and mental health. Taking care of my ethereal health was important to help me lift the veil to uncover my authentic self.

The below meditations and rituals are ways you can change and take care of your ethereal body so that you can affect the physical world around you.

Cord Cutting

Cord cutting is a type of ritual designed to remove the ties that bind two people together energetically. Use this ritual to help people separate from someone who is causing them harm or whom they are stuck in a toxic pattern with. (Adapted from the Revivalist site "How to Do a Cord Cutting Ritual After a Breakup.")

1. Cleanse the space you plan to perform the ritual in by burning sage.

   - Cleansing clears the room of negative energy and allows you to focus on your ritual work. Grab a sage stick or put some sage into a fireproof bowl, then light it and let it burn for about twenty seconds. Fan the smoke into all corners of the room for a thorough cleanse. If burning sage indoors isn't your thing, cleanse your space with purifying incense, a sound bath from a meditation bowl, or a large selenite crystal.

- Put out the smoking sage with water when you're ready to begin the cord-cutting ritual.
- Keep your windows cracked open while you burn sage so the smoke doesn't accumulate in your home.
- Set short candles about ten inches (25 cm) apart, connected by a string.

2. Gather two candles, preferably black. Place the candles in candle holders or in small bowls filled with sea salt to hold them upright. Tie a piece of string or twine around the middle of one candle, then tie the other end around the other candle. Pull the candles apart until the string is tight.

- Use a color other than black if black isn't available (for example, if the other person's favorite color is blue, blue candles will work).
- If you're using bowls with sea salt, make sure the bowls are made of a fireproof material like stainless steel, ceramic, or glass.
- Since the candles may burn for several hours, set them in an open spot that's safe away from clutter.

3. Set an intention to cut ties and thank the person for what you've learned.

- Take a few moments to meditate or do some deep breathing to focus your energy. Think about the person, relationship, place, or idea that you want to separate from and reflect on how holding space for them drains your energy. Thank the person (out loud or silently) for the lessons you've learned from their presence in your life.
- Cut cords with a whole person if you want to completely release their energy from your life. Otherwise, cut cords with an aspect of your relationship to keep them in your

life (for example, if you want to release someone as a lover but keep them as a friend).

4. Light the candles and declare you want to release the person's energy.

- Say something along the lines of "I release this person's energy from my heart" out loud as you light both candles (the exact wording is flexible as long as your intention to let them go is clear). As the candles burn down, the string will catch fire and burn. This is a physical representation of your energetic bonds to the person fading away.

- Some choose to end the ritual once the string is burned, while others prefer to wait until the candles are entirely spent (chime candles usually take two to two-and-a-half hours to burn completely).

- There may be some sparking as the flame reaches the string, so monitor your candles closely.

5. Dispose of the burned string in a natural water source to end the ritual.

- Take the ash and burned bits of the string and place them in a small container (if you supported your candles with sea salt, add the salt, too). Go to a natural water source like a stream or pond and release the burned string to close your space and end the cord-cutting ritual. If there's no water nearby, use a sink or toilet.

- Some prefer to end the ritual with a mantra about releasing the past as they discard the string. Say something like "I accept that others may not share my path or desires" or "I release my expectations to open myself to the wonders of the universe."

Grounding Meditation and Visualization

Grounding is a good way to get in touch with the Earth and therefore with the divine sacred feminine. By ensuring your connection to the bigger picture, you give yourself a chance to release the active stressors of your life and allow yourself to show up with security and acceptance.

Find a quiet place to sit. Suggested places to find would be in nature, by water, in the sunlight, near a fountain, near a windchime, or anywhere you can feel at peace. Some people even make their closet into their meditation room and include an altar. Closets can be great for many things besides being trapped in them.

Once you find your place, put some soft, soothing music on and close your eyes. You might want to find a pillow to sit on to make it more comfortable for a longer meditation.

Imagine a white cord coming from the sky through the top of your head. Imagine it going through the crown of your head all of the way down to the end of your spine connecting you to Mother Earth. Imagine Mother Earth supporting you and providing you with all that you need. Take three deep breaths and while you inhale imagine red, purple, and green light coming into your spine and nervous system from the Earth. See the red, purple, and green light spiral into your spine, relaxing the nervous system and giving you life. Then imagine the red, purple, and green light spiraling up the spine into the crown of your head up into the sky. Do this visualization rotation three times or as often as needed to help ground your energy.

Say this affirmation along with the visualization for added benefit.

"Mother Earth always takes care of me and provides for me. I don't need to push things or force the natural flow because the Mother takes care of me like a mother would take care of her child. Even if my biological mother has not taken care of me, the sacred feminine's perfect love for me will not let me down. She loves and cares for me unconditionally."

Chakra Meditations

Doing meditations to open your chakras can be good for unblocking certain aspects of life connected to the specific areas of your body. If you are looking to get back in touch with the divine masculine or feminine, focus your attention on the lower chakra points during your meditations. It will help you align with that divine aspect of the self.

Find a quiet place to meditate as you did for the grounding meditation.

Start some soothing music and close your eyes. Inhale and exhale three times to center yourself.

Imagine a white light coming down from the sky/heaven and entering the crown of your head which is the crown chakra. See the white light opening your mind and helping to brighten the dark places of your mind.

Then imagine the white light moving to your third eye (the space in your forehead in between your physical two eye-brows). This is where your psychic ability and clairvoyance lie. Imagine the white light opening and expanding the third eye chakra, filling your thoughts and visions with white light.

Allow the white light to move into your throat chakra, located at the base of the throat. See the white light opening your throat and clearing out any words, expressions, or communication that has been stuck there.

See the white light move into the heart chakra located in the center of your chest. Imagine it growing and expanding your heart, bringing love and light to people who have either hurt you or you have unintentionally hurt. Allow the white light to grow your heart just like pumping blood into your heart would. Feel it start to heal past wounds, fear, and sadness you have experienced. Imagine it growing stronger with every light beam that glimmers in your heart chakra.

Now see the light move into the solar plexus where the solar plexus chakra is. This holds your willpower, motivation, and confidence. See the light beam grow large as it expands out of your solar plexus chakra. Imagine yourself getting stronger, braver, and more confident.

See the light beam travel down to your creative sexual (sacral) chakra located right above the sexual organs. This is where you birth ideas, creative expression, procreate, and experience sexual pleasure. Allow the light to travel into your sexual chakra and fill it with lively creative juices. Feel the tingly sensation of having white light in your sexual chakra and allow it to feel excited and loved.

If you start to get gas bubbles or feel tightness, it may mean there is unresolved sexual trauma stuck in your sexual chakra. This would be a good time to spend extra time in the sexual chakra allowing some of the tension to release. Continue to send love and hugs to this energetic part of yourself until the gas bubbles cease. If you are unable to get the tightness to go away move your hands over your sexual chakra and imagine the white light moving from your hands to your sexual organs.

Finally, imagine the white light going into the root chakra which is located directly above the anus. Imagine the white light clearing out any toxins that haven't left the body. Imagine it flowing into the earth and taking any negative thoughts, fear, anxiety, and physical toxins out of your body and see them flowing into the earth.

See a strong white cord flowing from the heavens into the top of your crown all of the way through each chakra into the center of the Earth. Imagine Mother Earth taking all the negative thoughts and feelings out of your body and using them to regenerate herself, allowing you to become a clear channel and vessel for Father Sky's knowledge, guidance, and love. See the white cord as vibrant and strong.

Resources

Work with Me

- www.nita-marie.com (for fans and adult models, experienced and brand new, interested in coaching on how to monetize online adult work)
  - Instagram @love_nitamarie and @nitamarieland
  - Facebook @nitamariecoaching
- www.nitamariecoach.com (for women interested in becoming their own sexual goddess and private coaching on how to lift their veil with reference to my book)
  - Instagram @ohmygoddessses1
  - Facebook @thesacredbutterfly and @ohmygoddesses
- www.dogheavenllc.com (for my animal lovers out there who want to support our animal sanctuary)
  - Instagram @dogheavenllc

- Facebook @dogheavenllc

If you are currently in an abusive situation, call 1-800-799-7233.

If you are currently being sex trafficked or know someone who is, call 1-888-373-7888.

If you currently have a sex addiction, call 1-925-261-8862.

Links

- https://chopra.com/articles/7-chakra-meditations-to-keep-you-in-balance
- https://www.mindbodygreen.com/articles/the-4-types-of-intuition-and-how-to-tap-into-each
- https://www.wikihow.com/Cord-Cutting-Ritual

Other Professional Resources

Amy Cheryl—Creatrix of Women's Worth Academy (WWA), is a spiritual and intuitive mentor for over two decades providing the healing and transformation needed for women to live fearlessly and confidently creating their dream life from the Feminine Frame.

She helps women break free from the exhausting pressures, hustle, and judgments of society's norms to be their authority, realizes their innate inner power and voice, be in nourishing supportive relationships, and shamelessly celebrate their success.

She is a sought-after expert in her field of feminine empowerment, has shared the stage with global leaders such as Marianne Williamson, and is featured in several publications and podcasts.

- Website: www.Womensworthacademy.com
- Instagram: @womensworthacademy
- Facebook: Women's Worth Academy with Amy Cheryl

Tanisha Martin—Tanisha is a transformation coach and sixth degree Kung Fu Master.

When Tanisha had her first breakthrough (in just thirty days), she tripled her income and left her abusive marriage. The intense inner work required to have that experience taught her for the first time that she mattered and had actual power in her life.

Now, she infuses this hopeful message of value and empowerment in all she does, including her work with her Kung Fu students and transformation clients. It's not about being someone different, but about being our real selves beneath the programming and survival mechanisms we inadvertently adopted that hold us back.

"Transformation is shedding what you're not to reveal who you really are."

- Website: 7StarPhoenix.com
- Instagram: @7starpheonix

Emily Valdez—Emily is a medium and eclectic witch and owner of the Witch Project. She teaches modern-day and ancient Earth-based rituals to help align your life with the sacred feminine.

- Linktree: **https://linktr.ee/thewitchproject**
- Instagram @thewitchproject_
- TikTok: TikTok.com/@thewitchproject_

About the Author

Nita Marie is a women's empowerment coach who focuses on helping women release their inner goddesses by tapping into their sexuality and pleasure center. She also loves helping women become financially independent which translates into business coaching in various modalities including adult online modeling. As an entrepreneur herself with her rags-to-riches story of going from $20 in her bank account to a multi-millionaire in three years, she now owns six successful businesses and a foundation to help raise money for nonprofits.

She has been writing short stories for the past thirty-five years and had her first short story book published in 2023 with her daughter titled *The Girl in the Woods* which reached the Amazon bestseller list. She's happy to release this book *The Sacred Butterfly* as her first self-help inspirational book for women. And she looks forward to continuing to write self-help books for women, inspiring them to love their authentic selves and to embrace the sacred feminine within.

She lives on her ranch, which has become an animal sanctuary, with her husband, twins, and more animals to count. Your purchase of this book is helping to care for rescue dogs, cats, and horses safe and alive who would have otherwise been euthanized, as well as helping humans connect to God through animals and nature at Dog Heaven LLC. Thank you!

For more great books from Peak Press
Visit Books.GracePointPublishing.com

PEAK PRESS

If you enjoyed reading *The Sacred Butterfly*, and purchased it through an online retailer, please return to the site and write a review to help others find the book.

www.ingramcontent.com/pod-product-compliance
Lightning Source LLC
Chambersburg PA
CBHW060318100426
42812CB00003B/815